"This work will be of obligatory consultation for all those researchers new to the fields of peace and the family, as well as experts in the sector, as its proposals are fresh and innovative, for it projects a new system of family coexistence, as it balances the members of the family, moving away from the old myth of marriage where only one decides."

Francisco Gorjón Gómez, PhD, *Professor, Autonomous University of Nuevo León*

"This research work is extremely useful for those interested in analysing the structural problems of violence in the family and in particular in marriage. It even opens a window to reflect on the role of these institutions today, their constant evolution and understanding, all this will allow us to find the legal and social challenges facing our society to build spaces free of violence, gender equality and care from a perspective of building peace and human rights".

Magda Yadira Robles Garza, PhD, *Professor and Human Rights Defender at the Autonomous University of Coahuila*

Marriage and the Culture of Peace

This book provides skills for therapists and families to help improve interpersonal communication, promoting a new system of family coexistence and a refreshed concept of the modern marriage in society.

Written from a constructivist peace perspective, the book's aim is to reduce the high statistics of intimate partner violence that occurs in Mexico, arguing that the culture of peace and how it is born in the family in turn affects society for better or for worse. Based upon interviews from 150 long-term married couples, the chapters address the components that promote peaceful dialogue in marriages, such as assertive language, active listening, tolerance to frustration, and gender perspectives. Including accessible language and several models of peace, the book uniquely examines same-sex marriages, the role of children in marriage conflicts, and prescribed gender assumptions and roles in relationships. It aims to empower family members to move away from old habits and seek a more equitable existence in marriages and society at large.

This interdisciplinary text will be of great interest to family therapists and clinical social workers, as well as to students and researchers in communication and peace studies.

Cecilia Sarahi de la Rosa Vazquez is a full-time professor and researcher at Autonomous University of Coahuila, México. She is a member of the National System of Researchers (SNI) Level I and holds a PhD in Alternative Methods of Conflict Resolution. She is a woman, wife, and mother.

Paris A. Cabello-Tijerina is a full-time professor and researcher at Universidad Autónoma de Nuevo León, México. He is a member of the Sistema Nacional de Investigadores (SNI) Level II. He holds a PhD in Social Intervention and Mediation and is a PhD candidate in International Studies in Peace, Conflict, and Development.

Marriage and the Culture of Peace

Communication Skills for Families, Therapists, and Society

Cecilia Sarahi de la Rosa Vazquez
and Paris A. Cabello-Tijerina

NEW YORK AND LONDON

Designed cover image: © Getty Images

First published 2023
by Routledge
605 Third Avenue, New York, NY 10158

and by Routledge
4 Park Square, Milton Park, Abingdon, Oxon, OX14 4RN

Routledge is an imprint of the Taylor & Francis Group, an informa business

© 2023 Cecilia Sarahi de la Rosa Vazquez and Paris A. Cabello-Tijerina

The right of Cecilia Sarahi de la Rosa Vazquez and Paris A. Cabello-Tijerina to be identified as authors of this work has been asserted in accordance with sections 77 and 78 of the Copyright, Designs and Patents Act 1988.

All rights reserved. No part of this book may be reprinted or reproduced or utilised in any form or by any electronic, mechanical, or other means, now known or hereafter invented, including photocopying and recording, or in any information storage or retrieval system, without permission in writing from the publishers.

Trademark notice: Product or corporate names may be trademarks or registered trademarks, and are used only for identification and explanation without intent to infringe.

ISBN: 9781032074542 (hbk)
ISBN: 9781032074511 (pbk)
ISBN: 9781003207023 (ebk)

DOI: 10.4324/9781003207023

Typeset in Times New Roman
by Newgen Publishing UK

To God AΩ Thanks for all the love and blessings you give me.

To Ramón, Solange, Varek, and Dastan ☆
To Carmen, Salvador, and my Brother Chuy
Cecilia S. de la Rosa Vazquez

To Reyna, Dánae, and Ainhoa *Omnia Vincit Amor.*
Paris A. Cabello-Tijerina

Contents

Prologue   xii

Introduction   1

1 Marriage and a culture of peace   4
National and international overview of intimate partner violence 8
SARS-CoV2 pandemic 10
Side effects: Childrens 14
Peace actions: Mexico 17
Peace actions: The world 22
Studying peace in Mexican marriages 45
   The birth of a problem 45
   Infusion of peace components 46
   The problem in Mexican society 52
Conflict in couple relationships 54
The old psychological structure of the Mexican family 57
   Marriage in Saltillo society 61
      Same-sex marriage 64
   Baby boomer generation 65
   Millennial generation 67
Reflection questions 68

2 Skill 1: Assertive language   77
The beginning of language 77
Linguistics, the science of language 78
The family language 79
Language as a reflection of society 80

Interpersonal oral communication 81
A glance at paralinguistic codes 82
Gender differences in oral communication 84
Verbal abuse in couples 86
Assertive oral communication 89
    Characteristics of assertive oral communication 90
    What to say, what not to say and how to say it 94
Neurolinguistic programming 98
Reflection questions skill 1 101

3 Skill 2: Active listening   104
    The art of listening 104
        Hear or listen 106
    Active listening 110
        Benefits of active listening 112
    Silence 114
        Learning to be silent 116
        Peace of mind 119
    Attention and understanding (mindfulness) 121
    Reflection questions 127

4 Skill 3: Tolerance to frustration   130
    Low frustration tolerance and violence 130
        An approach to frustration–aggression theory 133
        How to be tolerant of frustration 135
    Understanding stress 137
        The emotions of stress 140
        Stress typology and stress management 143
    Individual optimism 145
        Optimistic readiness for change 147
    Reflection questions 151

5 Culture of peace with an approach to the gender perspective in marriage   154
    Nature of the culture of peace 154
        Concept and evolution of the culture of peace 156
        The typology of peace in the twenty-first century 163

Gender and the culture of peace 169
   New masculinities 173
   Women and peace 177
Toward a culture of peace in marriage 181
   The care 184
Toward an imperfect and neutral peace in marriage 186
Children and the new generation of peace 189
Reflection questions 191

Index   194

Prologue

The volume we have in our hands today is the product of a high-level scientific exercise by the authors, which is framed within the construct of the scientific nature of conflict resolution methods (ADR), where peace is one of its main intangibles. ADR, especially mediation, is currently considered a profession and an emerging social science, derived from research and the approach and resolution of conflicts that scientifically propose a better social environment to ensure a better specific life scheme, as in the case of this work, on the institution of marriage and the resolution of its conflicts.

Dr. Cecilia de la Rosa and Dr. Paris Cabello are humanist social researchers who have dedicated their professional lives to promoting peace in their environment, in their area of influence and now in the world of social research. It is important to note that this is not their first formal exercise in generating knowledge, as during their research in America and Europe, they published articles indexed in prestigious journals on this subject, and these are the prelude to this work, which proposes peace as a pillar of marriage and a test of social stability.

The themes addressed in this book are highly topical; they deal with a social need, which makes it an obligation to study and disseminate research on this need. It is a great idea to propose peace and techniques for its application as a way toward the reconciliation and salvation of the institution of marriage, since the institution is in crisis due to accelerated social changes, where marriage has moved away from being the generating cell of the family and consequently of society.

The two authors approach the family conceptually from an ecumenical stance and historically mark its development from an epochal perspective, highlighting the so-called baby boomer generation and analyzing marriage in its most modern guise with the consequences that this implies. This new way of looking at marriage has generated a profound institutional instability, which is why equally profound measures are required to save and stabilize it, and this may be done through ADR, which are considered to be tools of peace.

The book highlights communication as a key element of a successful marriage. The use of assertive language is an element or medicine of conflict, but it is also an ingredient of positive peace, of the durability of marriage, of the longevity of a relationship and of the transmission of love between family members. To deny that communication is a factor in the success of any relationship has been a historical error in our societies, so paying attention to educating couples in marriage and all those involved in it about assertive language techniques will help recover the social mission of marriage, as our authors assertively emphasize.

Another of the great successes of this work is its approach to active listening. This is a technique known by mediators and one frequently used in all mediation procedures, which has a fundamental role in the solution of any conflict, so its approach as a scheme of married life is totally possible and will ensure the healthy coexistence of all its members. While silence is not the best way to run a marriage, it is true that learning to be silent is also a way to solve conflicts; however, it is not the best way to resolve them. Using these methods of conflict prevention and resolution can generate peace of mind, which is fundamental to making marriage a successful institution, so that all those involved pay attention to their life together and understand each other, because although they are not all the same, they are united by a common idea: the family that is the product of marriage.

The authors also address such important issues as frustration tolerance, violence and stress, all of which are triggers of intra-family conflicts that are the order of the day in every modern relationship; highlighting not only their effects but also how to cope with them and, more importantly, how to solve them. They even dare to propose self-composing formulas that will prevent their transcendence as positive peace measures.

Peace matters are the center of this work, where it transmits the great need to promote peace, to generate a culture of peace and how this is born in the bosom of the family and in turn grows exponentially in society. But the effect can be negative if this positive peace is not transmitted and the family is left to its own devices, causing social disenchantment and lethargic family growth as a breeding ground for the negative. For this reason, the family is not only the cell of society but also the gene of social peace.

The authors masterfully address the cutting-edge issue of gender and the culture of peace, as well as how the new identities and roles recognized socially and legally play a part in the family scenario, transcending just the nuclear relationship. With the new identities and role of women, the new masculinities have transformed the institution of marriage, so we will obviously have to adapt, and the institution of marriage itself will also have to adapt socially, politically, economically and legally, but to have peace as the beginning and the end of all relationships as a guiding principle to these cross-cutting concepts.

This work will be a vital resource for all those researchers new to the fields of peace and the family, as well as experts in the sector, as its proposals are fresh and innovative, as it projects a new system of family coexistence and as it balances the members of the family, moving away from the old myth of marriage where only one person makes the decisions. The type of marriage they propose is a team effort, one that is balanced, empowering all members of the family, giving vitality to the institution of marriage and ensuring its medium- and long-term future, an imperative need to get out of the comfort of the kind of marriage that is so common nowadays.

Good luck for this masterful work. Let us rejoice because the social sciences have produced today a way of better social coexistence and an undeniable evolution of the modern family. Congratulations for all your effort and creativity.

Dr. Francisco Gorjón Gómez
Monterrey, N.L. invierno de 2017

Introduction

The family is a fundamental element in the formation, teaching, practice and consolidation of peace, as well as contributes to reducing structural and cultural violence by being a key element in the construction of a social fabric capable of peacefully transforming its conflicts and thereby improving coexistence among all members.

For this reason, we consider it important to conduct a study that supports pacifist empowerment in the institution of marriage. How can coexistence in marriage be improved? That may be one of the first questions couples ask themselves when their relationship becomes difficult and conflicts appear that can threaten the harmony and tranquility in their marriage. The most common conflicts in marriage are simple to identify; they may be due to incompatibility, economic problems or poor communication. This book addresses the subject of communication as one of the strategies for building the culture of peace. It seems easy to communicate with someone else. We do it verbally, nonverbally and paraverbally; we are communicative beings by nature. Communicate is the preferred advice for those recently married, but the reality is that many of the conflicts that arise in daily life escalate quickly and quietly to become a difficult problem to resolve for the simple reason that no one has taught us the right way to establish a dialogue in which assertive styles are involved.

It is evident that there are couples who have experienced situations of physical, psychological and sexual violence that end in the death of one of the members, and also, in contrast, there are couples where respect is sought, and there is good treatment and

DOI: 10.4324/9781003207023-1

support for creating spaces of peaceful coexistence. This prompted us to conduct a study on the analysis of three components that favor a peaceful dialogue in order to be able to replicate them to support the construction of peace in marriages. For this reason, we decided to study couples who have been married for over 20 years to understand their dynamics and the strategies that they have developed to strengthen their marriage.

Latin America has been identified as one of the most violent and inequitable regions in the world, and one of the prevalent types of violence is domestic violence. In view of the statistics on emotional violence through verbal communication between couples and in marriages in the world, the problem was attributed to a deficit of peace components in individuals, an issue that needs to be addressed, so that in peace research, on way to study peace is to propose ideas or suggestions for peace building. The objective was to find those components that serve as catalysts and promote the culture of peace, thereby preventing the phenomenon of violence.

The results achieved are presented in this first work consisting of five chapters. The first chapter covers everything related to the origin, background and nature of the concepts of marriage and the culture of peace, as well as the beginnings of peace research studies, and peace work carried out in the world and México. The next three chapters describe the three components found in long-standing marriages: assertive language, active listening and tolerance to frustration. Chapter 2, on assertive language, discusses the beginning of language, the science of linguistics, the relevance of the family language, language as a reflection of society, interpersonal oral communication, paralinguistic codes, gender differences in communication, verbal abuse, assertive oral communication, characteristics of assertive oral communication and neurolinguistic programming. In chapter 3, on active listening, the differences between hearing and listening are presented, as well as the nature of active listening. The different definitions of active listening that exist are described as well as its benefits, and also discussed are silence, learning to be silent, mindfulness, silence for peace of mind, in addition to attention and understanding.

In Chapter 4, on tolerance to frustration, a review is presented of the theory of frustration and aggression, techniques for tolerating frustration are offered and the nature of its two indicators is described: stress management and an optimistic disposition to change. Chapter 5 deals more deeply with the culture of peace from a gender perspective, presenting proposals of different authors aimed at achieving gender equality, applying the ethics of care to the couple and new masculinities for the purpose of achieving constant participation, which requires the daily building of an imperfect peace within marriage.

This book is written in a simple way to make it easy to understand. Moreover, it contains abundant references to national and international authors that support the theoretical section. We hope that the information you find here answers some of your questions about communication and especially that this book is useful.

Chapter 1

Marriage and a culture of peace

One of the significant conclusions that important academics and scientists from various parts of the world came to is that war and violence are not inevitable phenomena in the human being. They formed this idea when they met and then embodied this idea in the so-called Seville Manifesto on Violence, in which many myths about these areas were shattered and used to establish a road map for the construction of a culture of peace through respect for human rights and fundamental freedoms by promoting values such as dialogue, solidarity, cooperation and empathy, among others, that make up a new, more humanistic and just thought.

The concept of culture of peace was introduced by the United Nations Educational, Scientific and Cultural Organization (UNESCO) in 1989, when it began spreading the idea of the culture of peace with the aim of creating awareness within a context that required an understanding of other ways to solve conflicts than through violence. Later, the United Nations Organization (UNO), in its Declaration and Action Program on a Culture of Peace, on 6 October 1999, explained the concept of a culture of peace as a set of values, attitudes, traditions, behaviors and lifestyles that imply respect for life, an end to violence and the promotion and practice of nonviolence through education, dialogue and cooperation (Muñoz & Molina, 2010), elements that we propose should be internalized and practiced within families, since the latter are the main engines of cultural change.

After several meetings and declarations were made, in 1997 greater emphasis was given to the culture of peace, marking 2000 as the international year of the culture of peace (Muñoz & Molina, 2010). The subject of peace is a preoccupation that is present in different epochs of humanity, with the first efforts focused on the construction of peace from a moral perspective where we find mainly religions. The efforts of these religious institutions were the precursors of the need to define peace from a more comprehensive perspective that includes both the absence of violence and the satisfaction of social needs. The need to have another vision of peace motivated the interest of authors who started defining new theories.

This is the case of Johan Galtung, who defined peace as the ability to manage conflicts with empathy, nonviolence and creativity. He points out that a system where peace prevails requires a culture and structure of peace, which is the way to eliminate violence (Hueso, 2000). One of the most important contributions of Galtung is to demonstrate differences within peace, categorizing it into positive peace and negative peace. He defined positive peace as the generation of a harmonious relationship; it is achieved when two or more entities in conflict undertake projects together and the benefits generated by this project are shared equally. Negative peace is considered the absence of violent confrontation, and the mechanism to achieve this goal is the resolution of existing conflicts (Galtung, 2010). The classification of peace proposed by Galtung has allowed us to explore and relate to it in other areas of study that have brought about the consolidation of a theory of peace from a pathological perspective that focuses its research on the analysis of peace itself.

Marriage in Western history can be traced back to between the sixth and eleventh centuries as a mixture of Roman and Germanic traditions. Roman tradition was based on the bilateral contract of mutual consent, procreation of children and in which the husband was to treat his wife with honor and social dignity; whereas, in the Germanic tradition, greater importance was given to the sexual relationship and the procreation of children (Rojas, 2005).

The word "marriage" has an uncertain origin. It could descend from the Latin *matrem muniens*, meaning mother and protection of the mother. Another interpretation is related to the fidelity owed to the father or husband. It can also encompass the definition of a natural mother whose objective is the common union of conjugal life (López, 1991).

It was in the ninth century that the Western marriage came about and the institution continues to survive today, based on the family unit "father, mother, children", its structure identified with the paternal lineage and the factor of love that unites all its members (Rojas, 2005).

Regarding the union of both concepts, peace and marriage have been linked since ancient times, because marriage functioned as a regulator of relationships and helped end violent conflicts. It was an alternative solution to seal peace and unite kingdoms with economic or political objectives (Mirón, 2014). As mentioned by authors in the past, marriage was intended to be based on the continuous intention of living together based on unity, honor, dignity and love.

From a philosophical point of view, for Saint Thomas, marriage was a natural contract, based on the consent of the spouses, and instituted by God, which had two purposes: the first the generation, upbringing and education of children; the second, mutual help, based on human friendship. Another essential aspect in marriage is the love between spouses. In the writings of Saint Augustine, he observes that in the goodness of marriage, in the union between a man and a woman, lies a good that manifests not only for procreation but also for society. The marital union is good for society in general, because the purpose is a mutual love. As Saint Augustine notes: true love, despite the years and even if the youthful aspect and the ardor of the flowery age withers, the order of charity and affection will link the husband and wife (Formet, 2021).

Saint Augustine, in his treatise on the goodness of marriage, makes several points on the conjugal theme. For Saint Augustine, marriage is the first natural bond of society, the first cell, which rests on: fidelity, children and the sacrament. Fidelity requires the spouses to maintain the promised faith and not to break the conjugal bond by committing one wrong act with another; children demand that they be received with love and brought up with pleasure and educated in religion; the sacrament asks that the union of the spouses be indissoluble, specifying that in case of desertion of the marriage, neither of the two can be linked again with another person. These are the three rules that regulate marriage, in which for Saint Augustine, the fertility of nature is dignified (Rodriguez, 2005).

By reviewing the Christian Bible, which is a set of writings that certain religions take as a spiritual guide for the adoption of behaviors that are correct, we talk about marriage; in the Book of Genesis, which relates the beginning of the creation of the universe, a higher being is described as creating man and then creating a companion for man, similar to him so that he would not be alone. With this history of creation, reference is made to the model that a superior being directed for the lifestyle of humanity.

In various books of the Bible, what the Higher Self indicates should be marriage is described. For example, in Ephesians 5:33 every man is invited to love his wife as himself, and wives to respect their husband. In another book, 1 Peter 3:8 indicates that the wisdom of the spouses lies in that they must be merciful and friendly. In another book, Proverbs 12:16 indicates that the foolish person will always show his anger, but the prudent overlooks the insult (Bible Societies, 2021). It is interesting that the relationship between love and respect is indicated, as well as words such as mercy, prudence and friendship because, as noted in the Bible, the culture of peace is based on respect for the other, on peaceful dialogue, which requires prudence, and empathy that is nourished by mercy and friendship.

The problem of violence in marriage may be due to a lack of personal skills that support a loving coexistence, respect, harmony and peaceful communication that authors have pointed out, which results in negative actions in the couple, actions that transform the good in marriage that Saint Augustine mentions, into domestic violence, which far removed from what philosophers and the central thesis of marriage indicates should happen between spouses and in the family. Perhaps this kind of violent reality that exists in marriage worldwide is evidence of several shortcomings:

- a lack of love and self-respect
- an immature human being who has not understood the purpose of marriage
- lack of awareness, positive guidance and understanding to raise children

- emptiness and a lack of purpose in the individual and collective life
- lack of knowledge and skills for coexistence.
- lack of spiritual practice that regulates and family coexistence.

National and international overview of intimate partner violence

Statistics in Mexico (Encuestas Nacionales sobre la Dinámica de las Relaciones en los Hogares, 2011) show that the violence against women is greater within marriage or by a woman's partner. In this sense, the aggressor is usually represented by the man. This does not mean that a woman does not have an absence of components of peace or that she reacts in the same violent way at any given moment. It is therefore premised that as a couple this deficiency is prevalent in both individuals, one for perpetrating it and the other for allowing it. Thus, the lack of components that favor a culture of peace does not only reside in one person but rather in the two partners in a marriage, looking at violence from a bilateral perspective.

The World Health Organization (WHO) conducted a study in ten countries, in which it found that violence against women is a global phenomenon, suffered by people in developing countries, in developed nations, in rural areas and in urban areas. The research involved 25,000 women, who revealed that husbands or partners are the perpetrators of violence against them, and this experience is reported as common and widespread. The same study revealed that the country with the lowest number of cases of violence was Japan, specifically in the Yokohama region, with 15 percent of cases, and the highest, with 71 percent, was in rural Ethiopia (Proceso, 2006). This result generates some interest in learning about the lifestyle and culture of the people living in this region of Japan, as they are the most peaceful in the world survey.

According to United Nations reports on the issue of violence against women, it is not confined to a specific culture, region or country, nor to particular groups of women in society. The origins of violence against women lie in persistent discrimination against women. The report mentions that up to 70 percent of women experience violence in their lifetime (UN Department of Public Information, 2009).

As can be seen in the statistics cited above, the female sector is the least favored in terms of experiencing episodes of violence by their partners; however, there is research that points to interesting data, in which the male gender is not only involved as the aggressor but also as the victim.

A survey of men in Central American countries reveals that men report that when it comes to violence, it exists in both partners, with verbal aggression or insults being the most common or frequent actions of respondents in the countries participating in the research. The type of violent behavior experienced by men with women as the perpetrators, is a push for violence, the same one that was mentioned when they assaulted women. Men indicated that the most frequent physical assaults they received from their female partner were: slapping, punching and hair pulling. In conclusion, men were more likely to be victims of violence than perpetrators (Pantelides & Manzelli, 2005). This type of study evidences the perspective expressed in this book, which is the observation of the lack of peace components on the part of both actors constituting a marriage.

In Mexico, as well as internationally, the problem of the lack of peaceful components within marriage is reflected in studies that reveal the high percentage of violence that exists, with 42.2 percent of Mexican women reporting emotional violence, 24.5 percent economic violence, 13.5 percent physical violence and 7.3 percent sexual violence (Encuestas Nacionales sobre la Dinámica de las Relaciones en los Hogares, 2011).

In 2011, the National University of Mexico conducted a study that revealed that courtship violence affects 76 percent of Mexican couples (Bulletin UNAM-DGCS-403, 2011). The report finds that, according to psychological studies, women inflict emotional violence on men in almost the same proportion. This aggression leads to constant fighting and even physical attacks. Often, men's violent behavior is provoked by their partner's verbal aggression in an attempt to release their anger or emotional baggage. The research refers to the factor of low schooling as a generator of violent behavior, but not a determining factor, as family contexts transmitted in childhood intervene, and then a cycle of violence is transmitted from generation to generation, reproducing negative behaviors and a lack of components that favor peace.

The revelation that seven out of ten dating couples suffer from violence in Mexico represents a complex scenario, considering this stage of the affective relationship is a prelude to marriage. It has been shown that dating violence can be a precursor to violence during marital life (Rivera-Rivera et al., 2006).

Until a few years ago, Mexico was the country with the highest levels of intimate partner violence, according to the Better Life Index, which analyzed several countries belonging to the Organization for Economic Cooperation and Development (Lara, 2014). A review of these types of studies shows that over time, the figures continue to reflect social problems that are of national, international and global concern. The confinement of people at home resulting from the pandemic by the SARS-CoV2 virus increased the incidents of domestic violence, as seen in statistics. In Mexico in the period from January 2020 to May 2021, the National Public Security System registered 326,634 cases of gender violence. The main aggressions that are carried out in homes are offenses or humiliations, with a higher percentage prevailing among the female gender, with 4.9 percent, compared to the male gender, with 3.2 percent, followed by threats to kick them out of the house or to have been run; having been beaten(or) or physically assaulted(or); having been groped (or), touched (or), kissed(or), or if he has been leaned over or stood close to someone without consent; having been attacked (or) assaulted with a knife or firearm; and finally, having been sexually assaulted (or). All these situations show higher numbers for women (INEGI, 2021).

SARS-CoV2 pandemic

In January 2020, the world began the year with news that would begin to worry all countries about a health situation that had never been manifested before. It was a disease that was causing pneumonia in the inhabitants of Wuhan, a province of Hubei, in China, which experts would later find was a new coronavirus causing hospitalizations and deaths within the country.

In Mexico, the virus appeared on February 27, 2020, when the first case of COVID-19 was detected, so the first phase of the pandemic began (Saénz, 2021). The virus quickly spread around the world. On March 11, when many cases began to be registered in different countries and the severity it caused in humans was discovered, WHO (2020) identified COVID-19 as a pandemic. Therefore, the Ministry of Health made the declaration of Sana Distancia Day, where health measures and distancing between people would be taken to avoid spreading the virus (Saénz, 2021).

In April of the same year, the country entered phase 3 of the pandemic. This was a year of uncertainty, disease and death. Many shops, entertainment and recreation centers closed because they could not sustain themselves due to the lack of people to visit them. Face-to-face classes at all educational levels were established online until August, when some private schools started face-to-face classes with permits from the Ministry of Public Health. The pandemic caused consequences not only economically but also in families and in relationships in which people were locked up together for the first time, living together almost 24 hours a day when they could not leave home, except for those persons who belonged to the sector of essential activities. These consequences of living at home due to the pandemic were reflected in the information that came out at the end of the year.

The year 2020 closed with the highest number of complaints of family violence since it was recorded, in total 220,000 reports or complaints. That is to say, 603 investigation folders were opened per day, 25 per hour, in addition to 689,000 emergency 911 calls for family violence, meaning there was one call every 45 seconds (Sistema Nacional de Seguridad Pública, 2020).

The second year of the pandemic, 2021, began with the vaccination for COVID-19 and the arrival of new variants, such as Delta and Omicron, of the virus that causes SARS-CoV2 being announced, although vaccines have helped slow down the virus and allow people to restart activities. According to the authorities, there are new waves of infection that have been caused by a variant of Omicron, which has the fastest transmission (Redacción Nacional Conecta, 2021).

With vaccinations in place, more people began to leave their homes with greater confidence that they would not end up intubated in the hospital. Although a movement began to restart businesses and schools and people began to leave home, the data and information on the end of the year regarding the issue of violence, were not more positive than for the year 2020. According to a report by the Executive Secretariat of the National Public Security System, family violence grew by 15.5 percent during the first months of 2021 compared to 2020. In total, 233,000 reports of family violence have been accumulated (Secretario Ejecutivo del Sistema Nacional de Seguridad Pública, 2021).

The phenomenon of forced confinement to which the world had to submit due to the COVID-19 pandemic was not only a serious health problem, but also, with people locked up at home, the violence intensified. Yordi (2020, as cited in Montero-Medina et al., 2020), an expert from WHO, indicated that reports of violence increased in all countries of the world.

A systematic review carried out by researchers indicates that in different Ibero-American countries, domestic violence increased during social distancing, in all its variations: child abuse, partner violence and violence toward the elderly; in different types such as psychological, emotional, physical, sexual, economic and child sexual abuse; with symptoms associated with anxiety disorders, depression and post-traumatic stress. The same analysis found that authorities sought help from various sectors to shape strategies to address such a serious problem, but since domestic violence is a psychosocial problem, multicausal with many variables, it must be managed urgently with actions of prevention, promotion, evaluation and intervention, through interdisciplinary and multidisciplinary approaches with teams that can guarantee the rights of people who have been victims of abuse (Zambrano Villalba, 2021).

The predictions were not positive, as experts indicated that as long as the confinement continues in the coming months, another 31 million cases of domestic violence in the world were estimated during that time (United Nations Agency for Sexual and Reproductive Health 2020, as cited in Montero-Medina et al., 2020).

In reviewing the rise in the statistics of domestic violence worldwide in all its dimensions at the root of a historical event such as the one we have just lived through, it reflects in a crude way that a change in humanity is required. There is something that is not working inside people; there are gaps that each person must be responsible for finding and healing. Finally, this book is about presenting the idea that the culture of peace in marriage requires skills, work, understanding of the importance of the union between two people and above all the consequences of this coexistence in society.

Below are a number of suggestions that are considered urgent to start creating healthier dynamics.

- Mental health diagnoses in people. After a historic event like the COVID-19 pandemic, it is necessary to understand the physical, mental, emotional and spiritual state of health of human beings. The statistics do not lie: stress, anxiety, depression that have arisen as a result of this new lifestyle that was forced on the population should be the beginning of creating actions that allow us to know how a person is. So immediate attention to the mental health of the general population after this time of the pandemic is vital.
- Initial education based on self-knowledge in people. This type of methodology could allow a person to begin to know their emotions and then be able to regulate and channel anger, anger and frustration stemming from various situations that may have occurred throughout their life history and that the pandemic eventually intensified.
- Promotion and dissemination of healthy, peaceful and harmonious family coexistence styles. A healthy lifestyle must be evidenced, and media, digital platforms and networks are a means to reach millions of people, so it takes a cooperative effort to show people around the world that family life should be based on respect for each other, regardless of age, gender or preference of any of the members.

- Encouraging and naturalizing the culture of attending therapy. Many of the reasons why a human being is violent are generated in a painful childhood, so creating networks of psychological support, free therapy could make a difference in generations.
- Empowering people with the tools for life in school. This allows them to face situations in daily life, engage in conflict management as a natural characteristic of the human being, understand this management and develop creative ways to find peaceful solutions.

Side effects: Childrens

Marriage, formed through a legal bond, becomes the family institution, the basic cell of society (Araque & Rodríguez, 2008). The family is one of the most important socializing institutions; therefore, it is important to consider this formative stage to promote the internalization of values and skills for the construction of a culture of peace. If the family is lacking in components that favor a culture of peace, this can led to a negative perspective that directly affects all the elements that make up the family. This is the case with the most vulnerable population: children.

Mexican statistics reveal that in 2011 there were 18,136 reports of child abuse (Sistema Estatal para el Desarrollo de la Familia, 2011). Ten years later, by 2021, in Mexico there were more than 27,772 crimes against children and adolescents, that is, seven homicides a day plus 107 femicides on average and 13,758 cases of injuries (Save the Children, 2022). These types of situations in which minors grow up in family circles with violent situations, turn them into individuals who will repeat the same pattern of behavior in adulthood (Secretaría de Seguridad Pública, 2010). Hence, there is a vicious circle that continues and continues for generations without stopping, and urgent social problems that must be addressed by various sectors. To counteract this, public policies are needed to help strengthen the social and economic supports for family members who reduce violence within the family and develop the socio-cognitive skills for the proper management of family disputes using dialogue as a potential tool for empathy, solidarity, cooperation and tolerance, elements of the culture of peace.

This problem of a lack of factors in Mexico can be analyzed from different perspectives. Tentatively, two perspectives of the positioning of the problem are mentioned:

At the *cultural* level in Mexico, the teaching-learning processes focus mainly on the transmission of curricular contents, leaving aside education based on acquiring the knowledge and skills necessary to grow up with the tools to understand a conflict and transform it peacefully.

Parents, mainly those of earlier generations, were brought up in a traditional way in which there was too much control over their behavior, so the idea of practicing continuous communication through dialogue with their children may seem utopian. Another characteristic of the conservative upbringing of the past was the strict, respectful behavior of family members within the family circle, with the titles "Mr." and "Mrs." used and the children not allowed to call their parents by their first name or in a more familiar way. It was also rare to find constant communication from parents of older generations where there was a genuine interest in getting to know their children and how they were developing their thinking.

At the *economic* level, Mexico is currently a developing country, with basic problems such as malnutrition, unemployment, poverty and access to health, education, housing and work. The most recent figures from the National Council for the Evaluation of Social Development Policy (CONEVAL) show that since 2012, 19.7 percent of the population has been living in extreme poverty and 53.3 percent in poverty (Melgar & Hernández, 2014). Given this type of situation the population is confronted with, it is difficult to inform or teach them how to solve their conflicts in a peaceful way and achieve peace building, when people need to eat to survive.

The difficult economic and cultural conditions that may arise in any country are a threat to peace building and may block the consolidation of peaceful coexistence in a couple. In this situation, the questions arise, Is violence part of us? Are we born violent? To answer these questions, there are different schools of thought that have generated and developed theories to understand how violence is generated in human beings, that is, whether we are born or learn to be violent.

In the case of the instinctive school, it maintains that the origin of conflict and violence is part of human nature, whereas for the psycho-sociological school, it is the circumstances in which people live and find themselves, not so much within themselves. For its part, the structuralist school reiterates that humans do not engage in violence in its natural form, but it is acquired through the society in which they live (Osorio, 2012).

In this sense, the theoretical basis for this book is structuralist thought, which considers that violence is not part of human nature but is an acquired pattern; therefore, it is possible to achieve a coexistence within a marriage, where conflicts are resolved through respectful dialogue, thus favoring a culture of peace.

This is in accordance with anthropological models that describe human beings as cooperative and collaborative entities, where solidarity, care and mutual support prevail. It is at these stages of learning that we acquire skills and mechanisms that help counteract the innate aggressiveness of our species. Aggressiveness is understood as that innate behavior which unfolds automatically before certain stimuli and disappears or attenuates with the appearance of inhibitors such as empathy (Sanmartín, 2011).

The pandemic caused by SARS-CoV2 that began almost two years ago generated a series of positive and negative consequences for humanity. Many people around the world had to return home to remain in confinement, which they are still living with even up to the present day due to the disease and the variants that have been triggered by COVID-19 that are still in our lives.

The occurrence of event in countries such as Mexico generated family conflicts that, because they were not managed peacefully, accelerated an increase in domestic violence, evidenced by the registering of complaints that were not seen in the past. It is from this conflict that arose in the pandemic that changes must be generated. This situation requires actions taken by humanity to learn not only new forms of work but also how to living with oneself and, as a consequence of that, the importance of living with oneself first.

Peace-building actions in the pandemic must be generated from the knowledge, learning and practice of life skills. This set of tools allows the human being to know, to explore his interior, to grow, to communicate in a more assertive way with himself and with his surroundings, and to understand his conflictive nature in order to give it the importance it requires without placing it at the center of his life.

Human development is no longer a matter of people who "have time"; rather, it is an urgent issue to be incorporated into early education, because there is a risk of continuing to naturalize violent coexistence. Therefore, we conclude with some suggestions that anyone committed to building individual and collective peace needs to start doing today:

- Invest in your self-knowledge.
- Find and practice what strengthens your internality.
- Do not prioritize conflict in your life; instead, learn how to manage it and give it the place and time it deserves.
- Calm your mind; learn to meditate.
- Identify how you communicate.
- Learn to know your type of listening.
- Manage your tone and intensity of voice.
- Learn to say NO.
- Learn to set limits with touch.
- Find a passion.
- Look for physical activity that is for you.
- Accept that you have an internal war. Every human being has it. Go to therapy to heal your wounds and grow.
- Do less criticizing, condemning or judging; every time you do, you hurt yourself.
- Be more grateful. The pandemic taught us that if you have health, you have everything.

Peace actions: Mexico

Returning to peace actions in Mexico throughout history, after the violent conflict of the past in the state of Chiapas in 1994, communities were severely damaged after losing all their belongings. In response to this situation, the "Joint Program for a Culture of Peace" was born in 2009, which was one of the strategies of the United Nations to address this situation through its agencies in coordination with the federal government, the government of Chiapas. This program was supported by the Spanish Fund, and within the objectives the program sought to promote a culture of peace, bring justice to the displaced population and improve their living conditions. The program ended its work on February 28, 2013 (Programa Conjunto por una Cultura de Paz, 2012).

Another of the actions to promote a culture of peace in past years was the Program for the Prevention of Gender Violence in Indigenous Communities, implemented in the states of Chiapas and Oaxaca from 2010 to 2013 through the United Nations, which promoted equality between women and men as a reality in everyday life. It also emphasized that violence should have no place in interpersonal relationships and that women should not be subjected to aggression or limitations in the realization of their lives, their rights, their public life or their intimate life for any reason (United Nations System in Mexico, 2010).

In 1996, Mexico issued the Law on Assistance and Prevention of Domestic Violence, which establishes the means and competence required by the organs of justice to intervene, attend to and take the necessary protective measures in cases of domestic violence. This law punishes with greater harshness offenses related to injury and those that threaten freedom and normal psychosexual development (Pérez, 1999). It was in that same year that Alternativas Pacíficas was created, an organization founded in the city of Monterrey, Nuevo León, Mexico, which was the spearhead for family violence to be considered a crime in the state and for the creation of an official standard—NOM-190—which establishes criteria and protocols for the care of victims of violence in the health sector (Pacrez, 2008).

Concerning violence among young people in courtship and by their partners or husbands in the country, the federal district government implemented actions and public policies aimed at preventing violent relationships among young people at this stage. Therefore, within the Chamber of Deputies, the then-general manager of the

Women's Institute was encouraged to develop a manual of behaviors in order for children, adolescents and young people to identify manifestations and consequences of violence (Asamblea Legislativa del Distrito Federal, 2013).

Another of the Mexican government's actions in response to the problem of violence within marriage or between a couple, was to identify factors that had an impact on it at the political level, and then the two most relevant shortcomings were published in the *Official Journal of the Federation* (2014):

- insufficient legislative harmonization and culture of nonviolence against women
- insufficient legislative harmonization to contribute to women's access to a life free of violence

The shortcomings identified gave rise to the National Program to Prevent, Assist, Sanction and Eradicate Violence against Women 2014–2018 (PIPASEVM). Of the actions that are most closely related to supporting the central theme, the promotion of a culture of nonviolence against women to foster gender equality is noted with the following actions:

- Promote permanent national campaigns on the human rights of women and girls.
- Promote the rights of women, girls, indigenous women, women with disabilities, migrants, adolescents, older women and women deprived of their liberty.
- Promote guidelines to eliminate the justification for violence against women in the media and advertising products.
- Promote the media's dissemination of egalitarian and respectful family relationships.
- Promote awareness-raising among media professionals on the causes and impacts of violence against women.
- Promote the recognition of best practices in advertising free of sexist stereotypes and the use of inclusive language. (See Table 1.1)

Table 1.1 Summary of lines of action

Lines of Action	Institution
Promote permanent national campaigns on the human rights of women and girls.	National System to Prevent, Assists, Sanction and Eradicate Violence against Women —SNPASEVM—
Promote the rights of women, girls, indigenous women, women with disabilities, migrants, adolescents, elderly women and women deprived of their freedom.	SNPASEVM, CDI National Commission for the Development of Indigenous Peoples.
Promote guidelines to eliminate the justification for violence against women in the media and advertising products.	—SEGOB— Ministry of the Interior
Promote that the media disseminate egalitarian and respectful family relationships.	—SEGOB— Ministry of the Interior
Promote the sensitization of media communication professionals on the causes and impacts of violence against women.	—SEGOB— Ministry of the Interior
Promote the recognition of best practices in advertising free of sexist stereotypes and the use of inclusive language.	—SEGOB, INMUJERES— NATIONAL INSTITUTE FOR WOMEN.

Source: Diario Oficial de la Federación Invalid source specified.

The program presented in the *Official Journal of the Federation* contains a line on action in which it mentions promoting the media to disseminate egalitarian and respectful family relationships. This is the only section that speaks not of just one person but that there are two people involved who create a family. Within the phenomenon of violence in marriage or with a partner, the woman is still perceived only as a victim, without consideration of the dimension of bilateral, non-unilateral violence mentioned in Pantelides and Manzelli (2005).

There is another program carried out by the National System for the Development of the Family (DIF) called "El Buen Trato en la Familia" (Proper Treatment in the Family) that has been implemented since 2009, which presents methodology and tools for the promotion of the Culture of Proper Treatment in Families. The objective of the program is to prevent risk behaviors associated with family and social violence and the abuse of children and adolescents. It offers advice on practices and relationships of love and respect for oneself and others in order to make children and adolescents happier, more creative and more likely to get along better with their parents, siblings, grandparents and friends. The program, active in several states of the republic, also deals with a series of topics that are closely related to the individual components that favor a culture of peace. In general, the program focuses on the family and not on the couple or marriage, which is the root of violence (DIF Nacional, 2009).

The main difference between the promotion carried out by DIF and the present volume is the specific object of study: marriage and not the family. The particular subject that is reviewed here is the study of the individual factors that each gender contributes to the promotion of proper treatment, which will allow for peaceful communication and coexistence; therefore, peace will be manifested on a second and third level within the family and on the social level, respectively. As marriage is the social cell, the impact it can have is reflected in the next generations, promoting a culture of peace within a couple by blocking the cycle of violence, making it difficult for children to adopt aggressive behavior patterns directly.

Actions have been carried out to promote a culture of peace through education. An example of this was when the Ministry of Public Education and the Spanish Ministry of Education and Science, through the Spanish Embassy in Mexico, signed an agreement in 2006 to provide a course-workshop entitled Educating for Peace, with the aim of training teachers with basic knowledge on the establishment of democratic values and nonviolent conflict resolution. Peace education is a positive action to start promoting a culture of peace; however, programs are needed that involve the family; political, economic and sociocultural sectors; the media; and activities that promote harmonious coexistence (Abrego, 2010).

In the same sense, researchers Reyna Vázquez, PhD, and Paris Cabello, PhD, created the first school mediation program in the federal state of Nuevo León, Mexico, where from the perspective of mediation between peer students, actions are taken to peacefully transform their disputes while acquiring knowledge and skills for the positive management of conflicts, competencies necessary for the consolidation of the culture of peace through Education for Peace under Conflict education.

Peace actions: The world

The United Nations based its Action Plan of October 6, 1999, on establishing activities to foster and promote a culture of peace for the benefit of the peoples of the world (Cabello-Tijerina & Vázquez-Gutiérrez, 2020). Therefore, it is necessary and timely to express the importance of focusing on studies aimed at marriage as the cell of society, because it is there where future generations are educated and can begin to show new possibilities for generating components that favor a culture of peace. The strategy of including values and mechanisms regulating aggressiveness and generating peaceful behavior in the family environment are important efforts to build more participatory societies, solidarity, inclusiveness and peace that will contribute to the structural and cultural changes necessary for the construction of the culture of peace.

Building and/or promoting the culture of peace is not a simple or immediate task; it requires a process involving many areas. It requires the beginning of self-knowledge, education and training, so that at the moment a conflict or situation arises, it triggers all the practice a person carried out previously and, in each situation, leads to a person applying the knowledge that has been generated through that exercise, preparation and training.

The construction of a culture of peace, as mentioned, is complex, although it is possible because, when there is a common effort to transform reality, nothing is impossible to realize (Labrador, 2000). The United Nations (1999) described a series of actions to be carried out in different areas such as education, human rights, economic and social development, equality between men and women, democracy, values, freedom of information, communication and peace.

Education

- Promote education for all.
- Promote education in values and attitudes that promote the Culture of Peace, dialogue and the peaceful resolution of conflicts

Human Rights

- Promote and protect human rights.
- Publicize the Universal Declaration of Human Rights.
- Promote equality in dignity among all people and coexistence as brothers.

Economic and social development

- Promote collaboration between people and countries to end poverty and economic and social inequalities.
- Promote social justice worldwide.

Equality between men and women

- Promote equality between men and women. This equality is essential for the Culture of Peace.
- Eliminate all forms of discrimination against women.

Democracy

- Promote democracy as an exercise of representation for all citizens.
- Everyone should be encouraged to express their views and participate actively in politics.
- Promote the partnership of citizens to better defend their aspirations.

Understanding, tolerance and solidarity

- Support measures that promote understanding, tolerance and solidarity among all people.

- Listen to others to get to know them better.
- Coexist amicably whatever others' beliefs, their skin color, their sex, their abilities.
- Learn to share with others.

Freedom of information and communication

- Ensure that individuals and the media are able to express themselves freely.
- Promote access to truthful information.

Peace and security

- Always try to resolve conflicts without resorting to violence
- Promote the elimination of weapons.
- Solve problems arising after conflicts (migration, displacement).
- Promote greater participation of women in conflict resolution.

Galtung indicates that the existence of conflict does not mean the absence of peace, and proposes that the formula for peace requires empathy, creativity and nonviolence; that empathy is required to understand the passions of the other, without agreeing with all this; that creativity as the ability to open new paths; and that nonviolence as indicated by the Dalai Lama has two directions: if you can help and if you cannot, at least do not harm the person (Jimenez, 2014).

The path of peace building is one that requires the intervention of different sectors, but above all the initiation of peace is an individual process, which requires the awareness that in every human being there is a war that needs to be identified, to be understood and resolved. When you see that everyone shares that same internal war that you are fighting day by day, it is possible that you can be more empathetic with others and begin to worry more about healing yourself than about hurting the other.

Other strategies have been designed that have helped identify the structural elements for the formation and construction of the culture of peace. Some of those strategies are

- a peace program: preventive diplomacy, peacemaking and peace keeping in 1992 (Cabello-Tijerina & Vázquez-Gutiérrez, 2020).

Following the meeting of the Security Council of the United Nations on January 31, 1992, and in view of the growing danger to social peace caused by acts of discrimination, violence and terrorism, and the increase in new demonstrations of nationalism, the sovereignty and cohesion of states was threatened by ethnic, religious, social, cultural or linguistic strife (United Nations, 2009). With the aim of increasing the UN presence as a preventive measure to prevent the escalation of conflicts, Secretary-General Boutros Boutros-Ghali suggested a detailed analysis and gave possible recommendations on ways to enhance the capacity of the United Nations with regard to preventive diplomacy, peacemaking and peace keeping, also adding the secretary-general would address post-conflict peace building.

The international scene after the fall of the Berlin Wall renewed the credibility and influence of the United Nations as a bulwark in the prevention of conflicts and acts of violence. To achieve this, the United Nations made efforts in the areas of:

1) Preventive diplomacy: this would include measures designed to prevent problems, to prevent the same problems from becoming conflicts, or, if they did occur, to prevent their spread; therefore, confidence-building measures would also be implemented between the parties concerned, more use would be made of investigating the perpetrators and the implementation of an early warning system to detect threats, where preventive deployments are used to prevent possible attacks.
2) Peacemaking: measures for the creation of agreements based on the Charter of the United Nations would be established using peaceful means for the transformation of conflicts such as mediation, negotiation and arbitration.
3) In the area of peace keeping, the United Nations presence in the field of conflict would be used with the support of the organization's military or personal police, who would be extensively trained to act in such situations, to agree on effective

measures to ensure that peace is preserved after the conflict has been resolved and to help implement the agreements made at that time and, above all, always be ready to help maintain the peace in its various aspects and confront the most serious causes that could counteract it.
4) Peace building: after conflicts would be aimed at implementing cooperative activities or projects that would help the parties to conflict to build trust and mutual benefit between them, all of this helping to prevent the conflict from recurring over time.
5) The efforts of the United Nations have helped maintain at times a certain balance in international relations; however, much remains to be done to positively transform the most common causes of international crises, economic desperation, social injustice and political oppression (United Nations, 2009).

- *The Year of Tolerance (1995)*

UNESCO Member States adopted the Declaration of Principles on Tolerance as a strategy to strengthen peace building, establishing respect for peace not only as a moral duty but also as sociopolitical combat against the increase in violence, intolerance and discrimination against people in vulnerable positions who are victims of their "differences" from others and that threaten the consolidation of peace and democracy.

The main objectives of the Declaration are to mitigate these consequences generated by "differences" and to promote respect for human rights and fundamental freedoms without the importance of "differences" between individuals. The Declaration of Principles on Tolerance is divided into six articles, which helps mark the unequal areas of tolerance and promote it in the different areas of life.

Article 1 states that tolerance is the respect, acceptance of and appreciation for diversity throughout the world, as well as the forms of expression of human beings; it is the way in which people obtain their freedom around their convictions and accept that each person works around their own, also by possessing the right to live in peace and to be freely as they are and what they are.

Article 2 is aimed at the role of the state in relation to tolerance, and mentions that tolerance must be impartial and fair in legislation and when applying the law and exercising powers, in addition to taking into account equal treatment between people and people having access to equal opportunities.

Article 3 speaks of how the existence of intolerance is a great threat to the whole world, so it is very important that each individual be more tolerant. In order to achieve this, it is important that socializing agents contribute to creating more tolerant societies.

Article 4 treats education as an effective method to combat intolerance; therefore, new training horizons such as Education for Peace, Education in and for Conflict, and Education for Legality should incorporate into their topics teaching-learning methodologies that encourage the acquisition of skills and aptitudes related to respect for the rights and freedoms that each person possesses and to understand the importance of these and can learn to respect them; in addition to understanding the real reasons that influence fear and discrimination toward others and being a help to young people by enabling them to develop fully, and, of course, improve the plans, content and capacity of educators so that the teaching of tolerance can be effectively included in everyday learning.

Article 5 talks about how, through programs and institutions, tolerance and nonviolence are promoted in different areas of life and knowledge. Finally, Article 6, in order to mark the importance of the spread of tolerance and to make people aware of this same importance, proclaims November 16 as International Day for Tolerance each year.

It is for all these reasons that the application of tolerance is clearly an indispensable factor for the construction of peace, since these two are so closely related that one cannot exist without the other, because tolerance is a virtue that makes the existence of peace (tries to contribute with solidarity and continue with human morals), allowing the culture of war to be replaced by a culture of peace.

- *The Declaration and Programme of Action on a Culture of Peace (1999)*

A culture of peace is a process in which trust and cooperation in people plays a very important role, since it is born of a population and is developed according to the customs, traditions, history and culture of each country. The culture of peace must therefore be based on the value that peace has for people and the way in which conflicts must be transformed peacefully, thus the culture of peace is constantly changing and developing.

That is why, with the aim of ensuring that governments, organizations and society are able to direct their activities to communicate, emphasize and give importance to the culture of peace, the Declaration on a Culture of Peace was created and at the same time the Programme of Action on a Culture of Peace was promoted, which should deal with conflicts that could lead to violence and take concrete nonviolent measures based on negotiation and countering the violence.

The program of action proposed by UNESCO to promote a culture of peace is based on conflict prevention and post-conflict peace building, which is why the activities proposed to be carried out in the culture of peace program provide support for the ideas of opinion leaders in a conflict situation, for the inclusion of minorities in the process being of help to strengthen society itself, for the use of the media to promote information for peace and cooperation among citizens, for work in developing an early warning system to help detect social violence and for various research programs on pre-conflict events, in addition to educating minorities and affected people on the basis of culture.

That is why, in order to carry out the activities proposed for a culture of peace, it is necessary to apply basic principles that promote support the values and behaviors of people in daily life which help promote nonviolence and underscore the importance of human rights and freedoms that each person possesses. It is also necessary to promote the way in which human rights are exercised on a day-to-day basis, to foster attitudes of tolerance, solidarity and understanding between people and different cultures, to take preventive action through the growth of democracy, to teach and learn about the forms of conflict and the ways in which it can be transformed peacefully and how to prevent the consequences it may bring, and to share the various types of information and ideas and not impose the same process for conflict resolution. However, this must be co-constructed on the basis of the same peoples and with the full participation of women.

In order for all these activities and principles to be put into practice, it is necessary to have extensive planning and implementation of national programs, to know what kind of issues need to be addressed so that societies can live together in peace, to establish networks that allow the exchange of information in order to create a space of cooperation and harmony, and to have the correct implementation of activities planned for the construction of peace within the organizations involved.

An example of the implementation of a culture of peace program was one carried out in El Salvador, which was based on the realization of various projects that marked the real needs and goals of the society itself for its development. This program based its activities on the importance of maintaining and recovering human values and practices, including the participation of the population, without leaving anyone out and educating people about a culture of peace.

All of this is closely related and plays an important role in the very construction of peace because it is crucial in the peacemaking process to keep alive and strong the values and knowledge necessary to maintain the proper course of societies. That is precisely the role played by the various programs of action aimed at promoting a culture of peace in the world, by helping disseminate and educate populations about the importance of a culture of peace for the very establishment of peace and inculcating various activities that can be carried out for it to be established.

- *The International Year for the Culture of Peace (2000)*

At the fiftieth plenary meeting of the United Nations on November 20, 1997, Resolution A/RES/52/15 was adopted, proclaiming the International Year for the Culture of Peace as a series of declarations, resolutions and manifestos with the objective that in the millennium that was about to begin, it would become a new opportunity to build, maintain and strengthen the culture of peace for present and future generations. Individual and collective commitments are part of emerging human rights or peoples' solidarity.

The Manifesto for a Culture of Peace and Non-Violence commits each person to respecting the life of each individual, completely rejecting violence, sharing the time and resources that each person manages by encouraging generosity, promoting freedom of expression and diversity in every part of the world, engaging in responsible consumption of the resources that each one possesses by seeking the balance and care of the resources of the planet, and always being willing to help the development of their own community, including all people, in the process.

The Manifesto 2000 is an essential activity in the form of the celebration of the International Year for the Culture of Peace, since it encourages the human being to take action on their attitudes and to be aware of them, in addition to helping make a change like a human being and to engage with his environment, fostering the spread of the culture of peace in today's world and being an important aid in the peace-building process by strongly promoting the importance of the culture of peace in the world and committing human beings to follow this same culture of peace (as expressed in the Manifesto 2000) and to implement activities that help in this.

This new positive vision of the world has had an impact by achieving the international collaboration and cooperation reflected in the Millennium Declarations and subsequently, the Declaration of the Sustainable Development Goals.

- *The Millennium Declaration (2000)*

In 2000, world leaders adopted the Millennium Declaration, which would then help set a course for setting goals to be achieved by 2015. These eight goals (Millennium Development Goals) have as their aim the commitment of nations to reduce poverty and hunger, to reduce disease, to eradicate the lack of equality between the sexes, to provide solutions to the lack of education in the world, to eradicate the lack of access to water and to stop the destruction of our environment.

These objectives are based on the Millennium Declaration, which states:

- Goal 1: Eliminate poverty and hunger.
- Goal 2: Promote basic education globally.
- Goal 3: Gender equality and women's freedom.

- Goal 4: Reduce the risk of child mortality.
- Goal 5: Ensure better maternal health.
- Goal 6: Contribute to the fight against sexually transmitted diseases and malaria.
- Goal 7: Preserve the environment through its sustainability.
- Goal 8: Promote the contribution of all in the world to development.

These same objectives, which help consolidate the commitments adopted by the United Nations at its various conferences; help recognize the connection between growth, poverty reduction and sustainable development; and promote that development is based on democratic governments, the rule of law, respect for human rights and peace and security, are based on measurable goals with actions that help monitor them and combine the responsibilities between developed and developing countries.

In addition, the United Nations system, to ensure that countries are able to meet these objectives, has designed a series of activities to support the strategies put forward. These activities are based on the creation of diagnostics and the control of investments, the growth of options and the choice of policies, and the strengthening of the national capacity that aids in facilitating better distribution of the services provided.

The Millennium Development Goals represent a significant contribution to the peace-building process, because by helping eradicate behaviors that pose a risk to people's lives and offer a way to promote solutions to them, they ensure access to a better quality of life for people (especially the most vulnerable and affected) so that people, by living in harmony and obtaining the necessary help to do so, ensure better development in the world and promote easier access to peace.

- *The Year of Dialogue among Civilizations (2001)*

It was at the meeting of the United Nations General Assembly on November 4, 1998 that a decision was made to facilitate and promote dialogue among civilizations, declaring 2001 as the United Nations Year for Dialogue among Civilizations; therefore UNESCO was specifically invited to carry out educational, cultural and social activities and initiatives that disseminate and promote dialogue among civilizations, The secretary-general was also invited to report on activities in this regard. All these kinds of actions are the result of the recognition of diversity in the achievements of humanity and of wars that highlight the importance of tolerance in international relations, as well as the meaning of dialogue in order to achieve understanding among people (General Assembly resolution, 2000).

- *The Universal Declaration on Cultural Diversity (2001)*

The UNESCO Universal Declaration on Cultural Diversity was adopted after the events of September 11, 2001, which was established to reaffirm the conviction that intercultural dialogue is the best guarantee for peace, rejecting the clash between cultures and civilizations. The Declaration insists that each individual must recognize difference in all its forms, as well as the plural character of societies (Stenou, 2002).

- *The Global Agenda for Dialogue among Civilizations (2004)*

In 2001, the United Nations Year of Dialogue among Civilizations was proclaimed, and since then the United Nations has invited UNESCO and other organizations to promote such dialogue through conferences, seminars, activities and school materials with the aim of developing dialogue. It is essential to know that this work must prevail since peace is an issue that remains fragile in many regions of the world. There exist poverty and conflicts that put human dignity at risk, so strategies must continue to be established, along with methods and actions that can save diversity and meet the needs of the most marginalized people (Matsuura, 2004).

- *The establishment of the United Nations Peacebuilding Commission (2005)*

Established on December 20, 2005, by United Nations General Assembly resolution 60/180, the Peacebuilding Commission is an intergovernmental advisory body whose purpose is to bring together stakeholders to gather resources with the aim of proposing peacebuilding strategies; direct attention to restructuring and consolidation tasks for post-conflict recovery; lay the foundations for sustainable development; and make recommendations for effective coordination between United Nations and non–United Nations actors to optimize post-conflict recovery practices (United Nations, 2005).

- *The International Decade for a Culture of Peace and Non-Violence for the Children of the World (2001–2010)*

The International Decade for a Culture of Peace and Non-Violence for the Children of the World was the result of a resolution adopted by the General Assembly on December 4, 2006, which reiterates the objective of strengthening the movement for a culture of peace, following the celebration of the International Year for the Culture of Peace in 2000 (General Assembly, 2006).

- *The International Year for the Rapprochement of Cultures (2010)*

The United Nations General Assembly proclaimed 2010 as the International Year for the Rapprochement of Cultures and gave UNESCO the responsibility to carry out the celebration, because of the organization's more than 60 years of experience in promoting and disseminating actions aimed at knowledge and understanding among peoples. Within a highly changing international context, UNESCO continues to develop strategies to create linkages within the diversity of the world's cultures (United Nations, 2010).

- *The Global Action Plan for Violence Prevention proposed by the World Health Organization (2012)*

The objective was to establish a set of priorities and strategies for action on the subject. With regard to identifying the components that favor a culture of peace, which is the interest being addressed, it mentions the following:

- Parenting support: promoting access to evidence-based parenting support strategies and related resources for high-risk parents.
- Life skills education: promoting access to life skills and social interaction education strategies for high-risk children and adolescents.
- Norms: changing social and cultural norms that are conducive to violence and promoting anti-violent norms.

In the strategy presented in the action plan, there are points focused on the teaching of positive behaviors in parents. The idea is good, but challenging strategies are presented without concrete points to address them.

• *The International Decade for the Rapprochement of Cultures (2013–2022)*

The International Decade for the Rapprochement of Cultures was born in December 2012, when the United Nations General Assembly in its resolution 67/104 proclaimed the period from 2013 to 2022 as the decade that aims to promote new ways of acting among diverse cultures and universal values. It aims to promote intercultural and interreligious dialogue, to promote understanding and cooperation and to achieve peace (UNESCO, 2016).

• *The 2030 Agenda for Sustainable Development (2015–2030)*

The UN General Assembly created in 2015 an Agenda for Sustainable Development that would last until 2030, which consists of an action plan for the well-being of people, the planet and prosperity, in order to promote and strengthen universal peace and justice. The agenda points to 17 objectives with 169 goals in economic, social and environmental contexts. This new strategy will last for 15 years. When adopted by states that commit themselves, they must establish actions and alliances specifically to serve the poorest and most vulnerable peoples (United Nations, 2022).

The 17 Sustainable Development Goals are described below, based on the justification presented by the United Nations (2015) for choosing them as urgent treatment:

1. END POVERTY

Poverty in the world decreased from 36 percent to 10 percent during 2015. Although statistics are positive and indicate a reduction in poverty, the COVID-19 crisis puts at risk the progress that has been made. New research by the World Institute for Development Economics Research at the United Nations University indicated that the pandemic could increase poverty for 500 million people. The pandemic would thus be the reason why poverty will increase worldwide for the first time since 1990. There are more than 700 million people in the world with problems accessing health, education, water and other basic needs. In countries like those in Africa, there are people living on less than $1.90 a day; therefore it is essential to ensure the protection of children and vulnerable groups living in poverty.

2. ZERO HUNGER

Some 135 million people are severely hungry, according to the World Food Programme, and the main causes of this situation are human conflicts, climate change and economic movements. After the COVID-19 pandemic, the number of people living with hunger could reach an additional 130 million people, that is to say, double the number that existed before the virus. There are now more than 250 million people on the verge of starvation, and humanitarian aid is urgently needed to provide food and world-class agro-food systems that can tackle this serious problem.

3. HEALTH AND WELLNESS

The global health crisis that led to COVID-19 has resulted in human suffering, destabilized the economy around the world and dramatically modified the lives of millions of people in the world. Previously there had been achievements, particularly in increasing life expectancy and reducing the causes of death in women and children. The pandemic has shown that preparedness is vital, so it is necessary to take efforts to continue seeking to eliminate diseases and health problems that are persistent and others that are emerging. This can be accomplished through effective funding of health systems, of health measures and access to life-saving medical personnel around the world.

4. QUALITY EDUCATION

One of the keys to getting out of poverty is education. During the last decade, there were great advances in the area of education, but there is still work to be done. Up to 2018, nearly 260 million children did not go to school, even though half of the children around the world are not achieving the minimum in reading and math skills. In 2020, with the COVID-19 pandemic, the temporary closure of schools was announced in many countries, which affected 91 percent of students worldwide, so by April of the same year, about 1.6 billion children and youth were not in school, and of those, 369 million were affected because they depended on school canteens. Never before has the learning, life and routine in children been so altered, which puts at risk the progress that has been made.

5. GENDER EQUALITY

To build a more peaceful, prosperous and sustainable world, respect for gender equality, a human right, is necessary. Progress had been made: more girls attended school, girls were forced into early marriages less often, more women held better leadership positions, and laws were amended to guarantee that right. There is progress, but there are still problems of representation in political leadership positions. Statisticians say that one in five women and girls between 15 and 49 years old have indicated they suffered from sexual or physical violence by their partner. The effects of the COVID-19 pandemic are evident in working women. This has led to longer working hours and labor in unsafe places. Almost 60 percent of women work in the informal economy, which puts them at risk of ending up in poverty, not to mention the violence that has intensified as a result of the confinement at home that has occurred due to the pandemic.

6. CLEAN WATER AND SANITATION

There are millions of people in the world, most of whom live in rural areas without access to water, and globally one in three people do not have access to drinking water; two out of five people do not have facilities to wash their hands with soap; and some 673 million people defecate outdoors. The COVID-19 pandemic taught us that washing our hands with soap and water can save lives, in addition to preventing the virus from being transmitted, so the problem of access to water remains evident because the current funds are insufficient to solve the problem.

7. AFFORDABLE AND CLEAN ENERGY

The world is moving forward on energy issues and is becoming more sustainable, and access to electricity is occurring faster in the poorest countries. The idea is to pay attention to the issue of access to clean and safe cooking fuels, especially helping in Africa.

8. DECENT WORK AND ECONOMIC GROWTH

The COVID-19 pandemic has affected millions of lives and endangered the global economy. The International Monetary Fund has warned of a possible global recession worse than the one of 2009. It is also estimated that almost half of all workers worldwide are at risk of losing their means to live. The economic and financial disruptions resulting from the pandemic are now causing high prices for basic commodities that people need to sustain themselves.

9. INDUSTRY, INNOVATION AND INFRASTRUCTURE

Worldwide, growth in the manufacturing sector has slowed; this happened before the COVID-19 pandemic, triggering disruptions in global value chains and product supply. Inclusive and sustainable industrialization results in economic strength and dynamism that favors the generation of jobs, thus increasing the income of people. These actions play a key role in promoting new technologies, international trade and scientific research. Regarding the communications infrastructure, more than half of the world's population is connected; it is estimated that since 2019, 96.5 percent of people have had network coverage, with a minimum of 2G.

10. REDUCING INEQUALITIES

Reducing inequality and ensuring that no one is left behind is one of the main goals of Sustainable Development. Inequality in countries is a constant concern, particularly in the area of income. The pandemic has specifically affected poor and vulnerable communities, highlighting economic, social and political inequalities. The increase in hate speech toward the most vulnerable groups is an issue that is increasing, so it requires attention.

11. SUSTAINABLE CITIES AND COMMUNITIES

The world is a more urbanized place, with more than half of people worldwide living in cities since 2007. The number is forecast to increase by 2030. Cities are centers of economic growth that contribute 60 percent of gross domestic product, and also represent 70 percent of carbon emissions and more than 60 percent of resource use. This process of urbanization has resulted in the increase in inhabitants in poor neighborhoods with inadequate infrastructure and services, as well as a lack of access to drained baths, which pollute the air. The impact of the pandemic was especially detrimental in poor urban areas with a large population since it was impossible to meet the minimum requirements of hygiene in people, as well as due to the need for isolation and social distancing. The Food and Agriculture Organization of the United Nations warned that hunger and deaths could increase in these areas where there is little access to food.

12. RESPONSIBLE PRODUCTION AND CONSUMPTION

Global consumption and production depend on the natural environment for resources that have gradually been destroyed. Economic and social progress over the past century has led to environmental degradation, which is in jeopardy.

Some data indicate:

- Every year, 1,300 million tons of food ends up rotting.
- If everyone switched to energy-efficient bulbs, it would save $120 billion a year.
- If the world's population reaches 6.6 billion people by 2050, it would take three planets to provide the natural resources to sustain them according to their current lifestyle.

Sustainable consumption and production are about doing more with less, about separating economic growth from environmental degradation and about promoting sustainable lifestyles.

13. CLIMATE ACTION

The year 2019 was considered the second hottest of all time. Levels of carbon dioxide and greenhouse gases increased starting in that year. Climate change is an issue that is affecting almost all countries on all the continents, which is having an impact on people's lives. Weather systems are changing, producing extreme phenomena. Although the pandemic helped reduce the impact of climate change in some aspects, due to the pause the world population had to make, this was only temporary. Urgent action is therefore needed to save lives and livelihoods.

14. UNDERWATER LIFE

Rain, drinking water, weather, climate, coastlines, food, the oxygen of the air that can be breathed provide life and regulates it in the sea, so it is essential to manage this essential resource properly and carefully in order to have access to a future. At present, there is pollution and acidification of the ocean, which has consequences for ecosystems. Protecting the ocean must be a priority for the preservation of all forms of life.

15. LIFE OF TERRESTRIAL ECOSYSTEMS

In 2016, the United Nations Environment Programme (UNEP) indicated an increase in zoonotic epidemics, noting that 75 percent of infectious diseases in humans are zoonotic. These diseases are closely related to the health of ecosystems. With the pandemic, the planet sent a message to humanity, which demands change.

16. PEACE, JUSTICE AND STRONG INSTITUTIONS

Conflict, insecurity, weak institutions and lack of access to justice are serious threats to sustainable development. In 2018, the number of people fleeing war, conflict and persecution increased to more than 70 million, which is one of the highest figures recorded in almost 70 years. In 2019, the United Nations recorded 357 murders and 30 forced disappearances of human rights defenders, journalists and trade unionists in 47 countries.

17. PARTNERSHIPS TO ACHIEVE THE GOALS

The Sustainable Development Goals can only be achieved through strong and cooperative global partnerships. For the program to perform its functions requires sharing the same values and principles, as well as the same vision that prioritizes people and the planet. Now more than ever, international cooperation is needed to help countries recover after the pandemic.

The United Nations has specific goals to achieve by 2030 for each of the 17 Sustainable Development Goals. Some are summarized below:

- Reduce all forms of violence.
- End abuse, exploitation, trafficking and all forms of violence and torture against children.
- Promote the rule of law and ensure equal access to justice for all.
- Significantly reduce illicit arms, strengthen the recovery and return of stolen assets and combat all forms of organized crime.
- Reduce corruption and bribery in all its forms.
- Create effective and transparent institutions at all levels that are accountable.
- Ensure inclusive, participatory and representative decision-making at all levels.
- Expand and strengthen the participation of developing countries in global governance institutions.

- Provide access to a legal identity for all.
- Ensure public access to information and protect fundamental freedoms.
- Strengthen national institutions through international cooperation to prevent violence and combat terrorism and crime.
- Promote and implement non-discriminatory laws and policies for sustainable development.
- Reduce the global maternal mortality rate to less than 70 per 100,000 live births.
- End preventable deaths of newborns and children under five.
- Eliminate epidemics of AIDS, tuberculosis, malaria and tropical diseases, and combat hepatitis and waterborne diseases.
- Reduce premature mortality from non-communicable diseases by one third.
- Strengthen the prevention and treatment of substance abuse.
- Halve the number of deaths and injuries caused by road traffic accidents.
- Ensure universal access to sexual and reproductive health services.
- Achieve universal health coverage.
- Substantially reduce the number of deaths and diseases caused by dangerous chemicals.
- Ensure that girls and boys complete primary and secondary education, which must be free, equitable and of quality.
- Ensure that girls and boys have access to quality early childhood care and development and preschool education.
- Ensure equal access for all men and women to quality technical, vocational and higher education.
- Significantly increase the number of young people and adults who have the necessary skills, in particular technical and professional skills, to access employment.
- Eliminate gender disparities in education and ensure equal access to all levels of education.
- End all forms of discrimination against all women and girls worldwide
- Eliminate all forms of violence against all women and girls in all fields.

- Eliminate all harmful practices, such as child marriage and female genital mutilation.
- Recognize and value unpaid care and domestic work.
- Ensure the full and effective participation of women and equal opportunities in political, economic and public life.
- Ensure universal access to affordable, reliable and modern energy services.
- Significantly increase the share of renewable energy in the energy mix.
- Double the global rate of improvement in energy efficiency.
- Increase international cooperation to facilitate access to research and technology.
- Expand infrastructure and improve technology to provide modern and sustainable energy services for all in developing countries.
- Maintain per capita economic growth in accordance with national circumstances.
- Achieve higher levels of economic productivity through diversification, technological upgrading and innovation.
- Promote development-oriented policies that support activities.
- Progressively improve the efficient production and consumption of global resources.
- Achieve full and productive employment and decent work for all women and men.
- Promote inclusive and sustainable industrialization.
- Increase access to financial services for small industries and other enterprises, particularly in developing countries.
- Modernize infrastructure and reconvert industries to make them sustainable.
- Progressively achieve and sustain income growth of the poorest 40 percent of the population at a rate higher than the national average.
- Empower and promote the social, economic and political inclusion of all people.
- Ensure equal opportunities and reduce inequality of outcomes.

- Adopt policies, especially fiscal, wage and social protection policies, and progressively achieve greater equality.
- Improve the regulation and monitoring of global financial institutions and markets.
- Ensure access to adequate housing and basic services for all.
- Provide access to safe, affordable, accessible and sustainable transport systems for all.
- Increase inclusive and sustainable urbanization.
- Reduce all forms of violence.
- End abuse, exploitation, trafficking and all forms of violence and torture against children.
- Promote the rule of law and ensure equal access to justice for all.
- Significantly reduce illicit arms, strengthen the recovery and return of stolen assets and combat all forms of organized crime.
- Reduce corruption and bribery in all its forms.
- Create effective and transparent institutions at all levels that are accountable.
- Ensure inclusive, participatory and representative decision-making at all levels.
- Expand and strengthen the participation of developing countries in global governance institutions.
- Provide access to a legal identity for all.
- Ensure public access to information and protect fundamental freedoms.
- Strengthen national institutions through international cooperation to prevent violence and combat terrorism and crime.
- Promote and implement non-discriminatory laws and policies for sustainable development.
- Redouble efforts to protect and safeguard the world's cultural and natural heritage.
- Achieve sustainable management and efficient use of natural resources.
- Halve food waste at retail and consumer level and reduce food losses, achieving environmentally sound management of chemicals and all wastes throughout their life cycle.

- Significantly reduce waste generation through prevention, reduction, recycling and reuse.
- Strengthen resilience and resilience to climate-related risks and natural disasters in all countries.
- Incorporate climate change measures into national policies, strategies and plans.
- Improve education, awareness and human and institutional capacity.
- Promote mechanisms to enhance capacity for effective climate change planning and management in least developed countries.
- Prevent and significantly reduce marine pollution of all kinds.
- Sustainably manage and protect marine and coastal ecosystems.
- Minimize and address the effects of ocean acidification, including through enhanced scientific cooperation at all levels.
- Effectively regulate fishing and put an end to overfishing, illegal, unreported and unregulated fishing.
- Conserve at least 10 percent of coastal and marine areas, in accordance with national laws and international law.
- Ensure the conservation, restoration and sustainable use of ecosystems.
- Promote sustainable management of all types of forests, end deforestation.
- Build on existing initiatives to develop indicators to measure progress in sustainable development and complement gross domestic product, and support statistical capacity-building in developing countries.

It has been a long journey, in which over time actions to promote peace have intensified, not only in Mexico but also at the international level. The concepts of a culture of peace, dialogue, understanding, empathy and cooperation are increasingly spread. All these principles become a suitable recipe for peaceful coexistence. In times of war, such as the one currently being engaged in between Ukraine and Russia, it is indispensable to continue creating new forms that allow the human being to find friendly lifestyles for himself, his family, his society and the environment.

Studying peace in Mexican marriages

In order to present an overview of marriage in Mexican society, this section aims to provide a better understanding of the phenomenon of peace as it has been studied. It describes the theoretical support provided by various authors for the selection of the three components that favor a culture of peace within marriage that are proposed, as well as the geographical and generational context to which the individuals selected for the study belong.

The birth of a problem

The problem of the lack of components that favor the culture of peace within marriage is supported by the deficit theory, which indicates that "if people cannot have healthy coexistence, it is because they do not know how to do so, not because they do not want to have it" (Burns, 2009). The lack of peace components makes it possible for emotional violence to develop within the relationship between the spouses. The daily conflicts of being and of daily coexistence require regulation of negative emotions, which, when absent, can trigger violent communication.

The deficit theory proposes that fights arise because of the lack of skills needed to solve personal problems. If people were not taught the art of communicating with others and solving relationship problems from an early age, then it is logical that emotional violence will arise within a marriage. The assertions of the deficit theory highlight the emphasis on training people from childhood in assertive skills, such as using language effectively and establishing a mental connection to real needs, in order to express their requirements adequately without these becoming part of a pile of frustrations.

For their part, behavioral theories have a similar foundation as deficit theory, as they make the lack of communication and of -solving skills responsible for violence. In the same vein, motivation theory explains does not attribute a lack of skills but a lack of motivation in people to the inability to solve problems (Burns, 2009).

The latest theory addresses motivation, which provides a different answer to the theories that support the problem being approached.

When reviewing the topic of motivation, some studies refer to providing adequate opportunities for participants to achieve the satisfaction of their physical and intellectual needs (Ross et al., 2013). This research found that in a study of medical workers, in order for satisfaction to exist, people need to feel respected and receive dignified treatment, enjoy healthy working conditions, receive fair and equitable treatment, not be manipulated and receive rewards for effort. As can be seen, motivation is related to indicators of satisfaction within the environments in which a person develops, which in turn are related to the quality of treatment and respect received. Giving a different explanation, motivation theory is perceived to be related to requirements that provide assertive communication skills and components, as indicated by deficit and behavioral theory.

Within the review of data, the common factor provided by the deficit theory, behavioral theories and motivation theory is that they all require tools that promote a violence-free dialogue that favors conflict resolution within marriage in order to inhibit and prevent openness to emotional violence.

In this way a series of components are proposed that can reduce the violence in relationships that trigger violent coexistence in interpersonal relationships. Therefore, the following are proposed as components of peace: assertive language, active listening and frustration tolerance.

The selection of the components mentioned above is a consequence of a review of studies on the principles on which the culture of peace is based, research on happy marriages or those with high degrees of marital satisfaction and studies on emotions, which are described in the following section. It was decided to propose as components those most frequently mentioned, merging theoretical foundations and proposals.

Infusion of peace components

As previously mentioned, the proposed components constitute a response to the lack of tools mentioned in the deficit and behavioral theories, a lack that generates aggressive coexistence within marriage and as a consequence leads to emotional violence through verbal communication, so it is relevant to understand the theoretical support that various authors provide for each of these.

Frustration tolerance is a concept created by Rosenzweig (1938, as cited in Correa, 2010) and is defined as the ability to put up with frustration over a long period of time, without trying to satisfy the motivation. For other authors, it occurs when the tendency to respond to a situation is maintained despite successive failures in obtaining the solution (Moreno, Hernández, & García, 2000); for Alonso (2005), frustration tolerance is considered an indicator of high self-esteem. In order to construct a definition that is easier to understand, we choose to examine the concepts separately: the concept of tolerance proposed by Nicolás Guardiola (2011) is defined as the ability of an individual to resist; while frustration is considered by Berkowitz (1969, as cited in Tironi, 1989) as the perception of a barrier that arbitrarily blocks the achievement of a goal which prevents the materialization of a customary reward, or that causes the realization of a hope to vanish. Therefore a composite concept defines tolerance to frustration as the ability to withstand a barrier or blockage.

Violence can be studied from different perspectives. Within the psychological sphere, it is pointed out that parents who abuse the most are those who have low self-esteem, who have a history of abuse, are depressed, have a low tolerance to frustration and have a certain dependence on alcohol (Díaz-Martínez, 2003). Other studies indicate that the behavior is based on ingrained motives, beliefs and values.

Violence requires the conjunction of other factors such as: a) biological—neurological alterations, endocrine disorders and intoxications; b) psychological—personality disorders, psychosis, mental retardation and so forth; c) family members—physical abuse, violent or absent parental models, family uprooting and so forth; and d) social—exposure to violent models, violent subcultures, social crisis situations and so forth (Echeburúa, 2011). Therefore, the factors that affect violent people are very diverse, ranging from psychopathological disorders, to the consequences of having been victims of physical or sexual abuse, to the repeated use of intoxicating substances or drugs, to exposure to the normalization of violence in various socializing instances.

Human rights are that set of powers, prerogatives, freedoms and claims of a civil, political, economic, social and cultural nature, including the resources and guarantee mechanisms of all of them, which are recognized by the human being, considered individually and collectively, and are based on inalienable values for a dignified life. Tolerance is a value considered as a democratic ethos in human relations, as it enables the parties to have a fair, equitable and balanced understanding of existing differences (Chica, 2007). The culture of peace is based on adherence to the principles of freedom, tolerance, solidarity, cooperation, pluralism, cultural diversity and dialogue (Cabello-Tijerina & Vázquez-Gutiérrez, 2018). UNESCO refers to and aspires to arm populations not with guns but with the capacity for dialogue and understanding, and to achieve this goal, it is essential to establish relationships based on tolerance and solidarity (Labrador, 2000).

Studies of marriages with a high degree of happiness found that the secret to a happy life as a couple lies in developing a tolerance for difference and acceptance of diverse points of view (Acevedo & Restrepo, 2010). Tolerance to frustration is the result of good management of stressful situations. It is one of the skills that define a socially and emotionally intelligent person. In order to cope with life, it is necessary to have the ability to resist stressful situations and to control our impulses; the two skills allow us to live in society (Oliva et al., 2011).

Unfortunately, we have witnessed that the new generations are characterized precisely by this intolerance to frustration, a situation that can increase violence in the marital relations they establish in the future. The family as the main socializing institution is being marked with these characteristics. For example, it is common to observe that in family gatherings, family members hardly interact with each other because they are immersed in conversations on their mobile devices, or they are checking their social networks, producing distractions in the care of their children that sometimes lead to regrettable results (Vázquez-Gutiérrez & Cabello-Tijerina, 2018).

In contrast, low frustration tolerance in adults tends to produce aggressive outbursts of disproportionate intensity. A small offense is intolerable and leads to exaggerated rage. Domestic violence could be considered a particular type of intermittent explosive disorder (Muñoz, 2005). Rosenberg (2006) is another author who emphasizes the importance of being able to tolerate both stressful situations and to exert impulse control. He says it is necessary to establish a connection with the real cause of anger or discomfort before acting, which are necessary steps to establish nonviolent communication.

As mentioned above, low frustration tolerance is characterized by inadequate stress management and is composed of three emotions: anger, anxiety and depression (Miller et al., 1994). So, it is perceived that there is a relationship between frustration tolerance and the emotions anger and rage, which favors violence. Studies indicate that when people get carried away by rage or anger, it can have destructive effects on personal relationships, affect work relationships and encourage aggression. The conditions for peace require anger regulation treatment, which is ultimately a form of peace education (Redorta et al., 2006).

Other studies affirm that keeping emotions under control is the key to emotional well-being; the art of calming down is a fundamental skill for life. Tice found that giving free rein to anger is one of the worst ways to calm it down. It is much more effective that the person first calms down and then in a more constructive mood, confronts the other person to resolve the conflict (Goleman, 1995). In conflicts, there may be high emotional tension that inhibits the rationality of participants (Redorta, 2014) and complicates the management and transformation of the conflict; therefore, we must reduce that emotional tension before proceeding with the conflict, and paraphrasing is a great auxiliary tool to achieve this goal (Cabello-Tijerina, 2021).

A research study conducted with inmates who had violated their partners revealed that anger control allows distinguishing, on the one hand, non-aggressors from intimate partner aggressors and, on the other hand, aggressors from each other, so shorter interventions focused on communication and problem-solving skills and anger management were recommended, according to Eckhard (2008, as cited in Loinaz et al., 2010).

Men exercise violence against women as a means of control, domination and out of fear of being subjected and controlled. It is clear that the social molding of how the father treated the mother permeates the behaviors and learning of their children and their future interactions (Hernández Castillo, 2017).

The fact that there is a variety of research studies pointing to the consequences that low frustration tolerance can trigger is one of the reasons why frustration tolerance has been considered a relevant component that fosters a culture of peace in marriage.

Promoting communication within interpersonal relationships and a culture of peace is considered key to success or failure in conflict resolution. For this reason, the components of assertive language and active listening were selected as two catalytic tools that reduce verbal violence. Peace education is based on dialogue, cooperation and trust; it proposes to develop potential and generate a culture of peace as opposed to violence that allows people's needs to be met (Labrador, 2000). As mentioned, the culture of peace, which has dialogue as its principle, requires disarming dialogue for the individual study of its elements, one of them being language, is perceived. For this reason, the use of assertiveness is proposed as the middle ground between passive and aggressive language.

For Ramírez (2006, as cited in Cruz, 2013), assertive language is much more effective than passive communication. Furthermore, it is a form of language that allows the building of a better coexistence without turning to aggressive communication, creating a better environment in interpersonal relationships. Other authors mention the importance of dialogue within the culture of peace, defining it as the set of values, attitudes, traditions and behaviors based on respect for life, as the end of violence and as the promotion and practice of nonviolence through education, dialogue and cooperation (Cabello-Tijerina & Vázquez-Gutiérrez, 2018).

For Barrio Maestre (2001), the dialogic ethos is only given from an interest in truth and this is when dialogue makes sense. Dialogue is absolutely essential to dealing with problems related to peace. Therefore, the use of the Transformative Dialogue is proposed. That is, a true dialogue for peace that fosters empathy, solidarity, respect, tolerance, the practice of nonviolence and social justice is practiced among the South African people, which allows them to overcome the tensions and suffering they experienced for many years (Cabello-Tijerina & Vázquez-Gutiérrez, 2020). Barrio Maestre points to truth as a fundamental characteristic of dialogue, comparable to what honesty is to assertive language. Levinger's 1999 theory of relationship barriers states that if there is no sharing, no talk and no honesty, and if there is monotony and disinterest, as well as lack of money and sex, both men and women, single and married, will be unhappy people in unhappy relationships (Pozos et al., 2013).

Another study on couples revealed that it is necessary to develop clear communication, based on honest and understanding dialogue, as reflected in the empathic ability to put oneself in the other's shoes in order to maintain a happy couple relationship (Acevedo & Restrepo, 2010). Two couple studies point to a similar type of language, mentioning clarity and sincerity as components of the assertive style.

For his part, Solzhenitsyn, the Nobel Prize winner for literature, stated that violence has no other refuge than lies, that lies cannot survive except under the protection of violence, and that the war of the sexes constitutes that violence which is firmly based on the lie that occurs in communication within the couple (Polaino-Lorente & Martínez, 2002). As the principles of a culture of peace suggest, studies on couples and on violence provide theoretical support to promote an assertive style in language as a component that curbs the use of violence within interpersonal relationships.

The last component that favors peaceful coexistence within marriage is active listening, which emerges from studies where couples interviewed point to the issue of acting with respect, which is translated into listening and controlling emotions (Acevedo & Restrepo, 2010). When we practice active listening, we create an environment in which the parties feel understood and heard, and that facilitates the construction of empathy (Cabello-Tijerina, 2021). In this regard, UNESCO promotes a culture of peace and nonviolence through education: by revising curricula to promote values, attitudes and behaviors that foster a sustainable culture of peace, peaceful conflict resolution, active listening and open dialogue, consensus-building and nonviolence in any of its expressions (UNESCO, 2014).

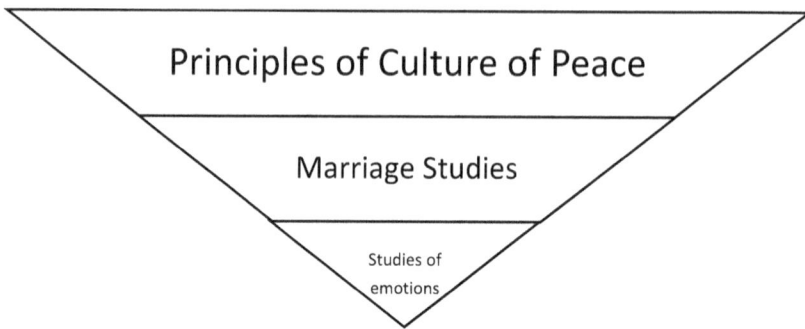

Figure 1.1 Component selection source.
Source: Niccolo & Maffeo (2007).

Webne-Behrman (1998, as cited in Laca, 2006) points to a number of rules that can be considered essential in any democratic group, which include the following:

- A strong commitment to rules of respect, manifested by active listening to other members.
- Honest expression of one's own views.
- Cooperative and non-hierarchical approach to problem-solving.
- Consensus decision-making.

As mentioned by these authors, there are a number of essential rules for democratic groups, which are similar to the components proposed in this book and that favor violence-free dialogue within marriage (see Figure 1.1).

The problem in Mexican society

The lack of components of peace in Mexican marriages, as mentioned above, can be understood by looking at the context of Mexican society and how it has changed over time. It is not necessary to review all the literature on Mexican society to identify examples related by parents, uncles, aunts, uncles and grandparents, in which they narrate how they were educated, and the social, economic and political conditions that they experienced years ago. In the past, education was of privileged access for some, the possibilities of studying for a degree were only available to the most privileged. Therefore, society lacked educational knowledge, self-knowledge techniques, assertive communication, sexual information and there were taboo topics that were not discussed in the family.

Traditionally, rules were to be complied with, as parents were beings of great respect and authority. Communication toward them was top-down, not equal, so they were treated as "Mr." or "Mrs.", so we can understand the lack of components of peace, locating a family context of rigid rules where there was no freedom of expression, no dialogue. and it was difficult to develop assertive communication skills. Based on testimonies ranging from engaging in physical violence when rebelling against the parents or by the father against the mother, to "stealing" women because they were not allowed to have a partner or to study, it is clear that those times were difficult to cope with in a society that is perceived as having deeply ingrained, inflexible and conservative customs.

There are currently high levels of violence in Mexico, with emotional or psychological violence being the most common type of violence in marriages. The concept of emotional violence is defined by the Comprehensive Program to Prevent, Address, Punish and Eradicate Violence against Women 2014–2018 as any act or omission that damages psychological stability, which can consist of: jealousy, insults, humiliation, devaluation, marginalization, indifference, infidelity, destructive comparisons, rejection, threats that lead the victim to depression, isolation, devaluation of self-esteem and even suicide (*Official Journal of the Federation*, 2014). These figures are the result of years of similar behaviors learned and carried out in the same way. The current context of a society with greater access to information, education, media and learning has made data and statistics available to everyone.

The statistics provided by the Encuestas Nacionales sobre la Dinámica de las Relaciones en los Hogares, 2011 (ENDIREH; National Household Relationship Dynamics Survey, 2011; NCHDS) suggest that almost half of the marriages in Mexico present this deficit, which indicates the existence of a problem. The other half of the population that is not included in the statistics, shows the real possibility of having a cohabitation free of violence. This is the sector that needs to be studied in depth or that may also be within a dynamic of violence but this is deeply naturalized.

Conflict in couple relationships

The history of humanity has been characterized by conflicts, whether between neighbors, family, peoples, or nations; therefore, the history of the human being can be considered as one of conflict, with ego, power, ambition, political or religious fanaticism, envy being some of the factors that prevail and result in the clashes between human beings (Múnera, 2021).

The problem with conflict in human relationships is that if you do not get proper treatment, you tend to level up, and if you do not know how to deal with conflict correctly, using skills, it is very easy to have violence as a result. This type of negative result cause the relationship to be damaged and eventually reverberate in all family members, causing pain and injury in everyone.

In Mexico and throughout the world, there is a problem of serious violence. The statistics in a country like Mexico are understood as signaling a structural conflict, which requires a long time and an significant effort to solve through many means, beyond personal possibilities (Redorta, 2006). The possibility that in the present we begin to implement actions and provide components that favor future generations to achieve a greater knowledge that helps the construction of a culture of peace, is a significant contribution.

To achieve solutions, we need to educate people more about conflict, know the reason for it, understand it and find treatment. Conflict has been defined by countless authors and from diverse perspectives. Fuquen (2003) defines it as an emotional state that is painful, since it is generated by a tension between opposing desires that trigger interpersonal, social controversies where resistance is manifested with stress, the result of incompatibility between behaviors, objectives, perceptions, or affections between individuals or groups that propose different goals. For Martinez (2005, as cited in Albert, 2013), conflict, according to its etymological definition, means "to fight", so conflict assumes that it is essential to human nature, understanding that this struggle with can be engaged in through violence or peacefully.

In this sense, there are authors who mention that, although conflicts are part of human nature, they should not be given so much importance in life. People should display a certain lack of respect for them, not being indifferent to them, but creating some kind of protection so that they do not become a reflexive repetition of constant thoughts that produces a brain block (Gutiérrez, 2011, as cited in Albert, 2013).

It is interesting that one of the characteristics of human nature is the conflictive being, because it is an essence that is not visible; rather it is invisible. You are afraid of it and you try to evade it. In the face of conflict, there are people who prefer to avoid it, without realizing that it will always be in their life, and, even more incongruous, they receive an early education where the curricula do not consider it as basic knowledge for human development. As Gutiérrez (2011, as cited in Albert, 2013) indicates, we must give space to conflict, but not make it a priority in life and, instead, use it as a compass that can be a guide to a positive change in people.

The theory of conflict as a social opportunity proposes that conflict is necessary for relations between people, identifies conflict as an opportunity for development, and allows us to demonstrate respect through the search for peaceful and creative strategies that enable us to identify the best solutions and not try to eliminate conflict (De Ocáriz & Burgués, 2014).

From the perspective of conflict as an opportunity for change in the human being, where this "struggle with" is used as a compass to develop skills and foster creativity to encourage positive change between the parties, one of the main scholars of the culture of peace and conflict, Johan Galtung, points out several premises that should be taken into consideration when addressing conflict from the transformative perspective (Calderón, 2009):

- Conflict is crisis and opportunity.
- Conflict is a natural, structural and permanent fact in the human being.
- Conflict is a situation of incompatible objectives.

- Conflicts are not solved; they are transformed.
- Conflict involves a holistic life experience.
- Conflict as a structural dimension of the relationship.
- Conflict as a form of power relationship.

According to Galtung's theory of conflict, there are three elements to consider in conflict, or what he calls the triangle of conflicts. In this sense, the analysis of conflict is about the interaction of three dimensions: attitudes, presumptions + behavior + contradiction. Taking Calderón (2009) as a reference, each dimension is described:

- Attitudes: how the parties to a conflict feel and think (motivational), how they perceive the other (with love, hate, resentment), how they see their own goals regarding conflict.
- Behavior: how the parties to the conflict act (they seek to solve the conflict creatively or to cause pain).
- Contradiction: has to do with the theme or root of the conflict; it is usually complex and hidden, because the parties prefer to focus on attitudes and behavior.

At this point, it is clear that a lack of focus causes human beings not to stop to detect the emotions and behaviors that are directing the conflict. That is, there is a loss of vision and clarity concerning what is really happening, concerning the root cause of the conflict, and that easily becomes an allowable way toward violence, due to not knowing the root that generates this lack of control and discomfort that ends up hurting family members.

In most cases, it is a complex undertaking to start this review and approach individually. Thus, it requires the help of specialists who can guide people to the beginning of this journey of self-knowledge that allows the exploration of childhood and the past, and that can help to find the wounds that need to be healed in the human being. So the process of building peace is a task where the intervention of several people is required. In the case of a couple, continuous observation and therapy are necessary to identify the wounds that generate conflict and that will inevitably be transmitted to the children if they are not healed.

Marriages of the future can be envisioned as potentially having greater access to technology. If in the present it is observed that interpersonal dialogue is increasingly replaced by technology and that more attention is paid to social networks than to children or partners, alarm bells go off to address the upcoming consequences that the inappropriate use of technology will bring to society; therefore, it is necessary to promote and encourage more recreational and family activities, contact with nature and coexistence free of violence where harmony, active dialogue, tolerance and respect are the way in which people enjoy and do not lose integration with their loved ones.

Therefore, as Ramírez (2013) observes, it is necessary to carry out positive actions in all those spaces that have to do with the social organization of families, such as the civil registry, the church and health centers, as well as the training of professionals who are in contact with fathers and mothers of families and governmental programs of social development in communities. As Elizabet Badinter (cited in Ramírez, 2013) notes, it is not only men who are jealous, ill-mannered and tyrannical; the existence of female violence must also be recognized. The problem lies in both.

With regard to this issue, it is essential to understand the psychological and anthropological perspective of Mexican society, which can provide an orientation for learning negative behaviors from childhood, generating the lack of components of a culture of peace that is seen as a problem.

The old psychological structure of the Mexican family

Mexico is a country characterized by great cultural and natural wealth, and general features shared by each of its 32 states, in addition to the peculiarities, differences, idioms and lifestyles that are in accordance with its geography and the productive resources that emerge from its very varied societies.

On the subject of Mexican society, which, according to studies, is distinguished by similar behavior patterns in old Mexican families, the author Rogelio Diaz-Guerrero established the psychological structure of the Mexican family in an ethnopsychology investigation, in which he combined psychology with methods of cultural anthropology to constitute the structure of the family in Mexico (Diaz-Guerrero, 1982). According to Diaz-Guerrero, the structure of the Mexican family is based on two positions, and is described in the following paragraphs:

a) The supremacy of the father.
b) The necessary and absolute self-sacrifice of the mother.

The results of Diaz-Guerrero's research indicate that from the birth of a child, there is already a set of expectations. In Mexico, a male first-born child is preferred, since the birth of a girl, unless it comes after that of one or two males, has traits of an emotional tragedy. According to the psychological structure, the birth of a girl for families of yesteryear was seen as a bad business, economically speaking: physical wear and tear and moral concern for the family, either in the case of losing her virginity before marriage because it would hurt morals, or in the case of not getting married, becoming a single woman, whose neurotic complaints represented a burden for the family (Díaz-Martínez, 2003).

One of the consequences of not having tools that favor a culture of peace is emotional violence. If we take into consideration the information presented in the aforementioned study, we can see that from before birth, the female figure is already at a lower level of value compared to that given to the male figure, an erroneous old belief based on gender inequality.

Returning to the Diaz-Guerrero study, it is throughout childhood that the signs of virility in males are recklessness, aggressiveness, roughness and not backing down, and that, above all, both boys and girls, must be obedient with respect to the family. In addition the boy must be masculine, but not as masculine as the father. The boy must flourish by playing with soldiers, guns, helmets, and any demonstration of feminine interests will receive severe disapproval. In contrast, the girl must grow up to be equal to her destiny: superlatively feminine, tied to the home and motherhood, should stay away from rough games, and should help her mother with housework, a taboo area for boys (Diaz-Guerrero, 1982).

It is understood, through the model of education that was followed in the past, that the origin of a violent personality in the male gender is based on the concept of a false masculine mystique, as addressed by Miedzan (1996, as cited in Fisas, 1998), which explains behaviors far removed from tenderness, understanding, delicacy and emotional connection with a partner.

Within marriage, the husband must work and provide; he knows nothing and wants to know nothing of what happens at home. He only demands obedience and that his authority is not questioned, that the wife submit to him and must serve him in the same way she saw her mother do with her father. In this way the Mexican wife enters, even before motherhood, the path of abnegation, denial of all her needs and the search for the satisfaction of all others (Diaz-Guerrero, 1982).

At present, changes can be perceived with regard to the issue of economic contribution, as women are steadily making inroads in the labor market and climbing to levels that in the past were only accessible to men. It is increasingly common to observe families supported by women and young people who, in trying to adopt masculine attitudes, are indicated by the cultural context in which they develop.

Regarding the theme of equality, the premise of gender equity is maintained in this book, but we have the idea that each gender has different conditions, abilities and perspectives. Men and women are not positioned in a struggle, but rather at the same starting point, where it is understood that each one has the same value as a human being, but each one has different characteristics that are equally enriching on a physical, emotional and mental level.

Within her ethnopsychology study, Diaz-Guerrero concludes that this type of psychocultural pattern of the Mexican family can be favorable to the development of neurosis. He also finds that Mexican women are often victims of neurosis, indicating that 32 percent of Mexican men over the age of 18 are neurotic, while 44 percent of women have this condition. The research concludes by pointing out that in the case of men, it is possible to understand the existence of:

a) Problems of submission, conflict and rebellion in the area of relationships with authority figures.

b) Concern and anguish in relation to sexual potency.
c) Conflict and ambivalence in relation to their role of being loving, tender, maternal and having feelings of guilt, and on the other hand being sexual and virile.
d) Difficulties in overcoming the maternal stage: dependence on the mother.
e) Problems before and after marriage because the mother's love interferes with the love for another woman.
f) The Oedipus complex.

The process experienced from childhood is very similar to the stories of yesteryear told by parents. This study, conducted more than 30 years ago, represents a psychological structure with certain similarities that remain today. Some of them are not as described; they have evolved. What remains is the emotional rupture in man, whose fragility continues to be restricted.

Diaz-Guerrero (1982) points out that during the first two years of a child's life, the child is filled with affection, caresses and love, and after that time he is prohibited from expressing any activity that does not adequately represent his sexuality, thus molding him into an already defined stereotype of virility and masculinity. If we take into consideration that the period from zero to five years of age is the decisive stage in the development of physical, intellectual and emotional capacities in a child, the most vulnerable period where self-esteem and security are developed, according to UNICEF (UNICEF, 2009), it is logical that, as Diaz-Guerrero (1982) observes, a certain number of Mexicans suffer from neurosis attributed to a cultural system governed by obedience.

For Cullen (1769, as cited in Rivera et al., 2007), the concept of neurosis is equated with that of nervous disease. Nervous-type illness is defined as conditions of stress, irritable bowel syndrome, fibromyalgia and chronic fatigue (Gómez, 2008). Interestingly, Mexico is the country with the highest level of stress at work, with 75 percent of employees suffering from this problem. According to figures from the WHO, of the 75,000 heart attacks a year that occur in people, 25 percent are related to an illness caused by work-related stress (El Universal, 2013).

It seems that we live in a time when families have evolved; when there are improvements in the educational system, flexibility of thought and greater freedom in decision-making; women capable of managing and sustaining a household, and so on. However, these figures show that in terms of health, illnesses such as neurosis remain, which Díaz-Guerrero (1982) attributes to a rigid family structure that has existed for more than 30 years. The revised study of the psychology of the Mexican family reflects certain primitive characteristics of this family, perhaps due to its ancient structure, such as abnegation and submission in women, characteristics that are not currently perceived, although the statistics on violence and its naturalization continue to indicate the existence of entrenched belief systems.

According to psychiatric studies, paranoid traits—mistrust and manipulative hysteria—are frequent in poor, uneducated societies where the feeling of guilt is a common tool. Unfortunately, in Mexico these elements exist with a greater intensity than desirable. The negative emotion of guilt in the male grows because of his need to express his vulnerable side. On the one hand, the wife asks for tenderness, respect and gentleness, but the environment itself prohibits and impedes the ability for him to develop empathic qualities for fear of losing his virility (Villa, 2007).

In psychiatric studies that point to guilt as a latent feature of societies with poverty, the naturalization of violence within marriage is reflected in the statistics of emotional violence and neurosis within the family, indicating the presence of certain structural characteristics of yesteryear that allow us to understand the origin of emotional violence within both husband and wife.

The importance of investigating the past, the history of a problem or conflict, is emphasized, because by identifying the origin of a problem or conflict, possible solutions can be generated. Hence, the phrase attributed to several authors, which states, "when you don't know your history, you are condemned to repeat it".

Marriage in Saltillo society

The city of Saltillo, in the state of Coahuila, was chosen as the location in which to carry out the marriage study on which the three

62 Marriage and a culture of peace

Figure 1.2 Location of Saltillo, Coahuila, Mexico.
Source: Niccolo & Maffeo (2007).

components proposed in this book are based. The state presents certain indicators of interest that differentiate it from other Mexican states, such as openness to same-sex marriage, the introduction of divorce proceedings and high statistics related to emotional violence within couples.

Saltillo, as the state capital, has 25 percent of the total population of the state of Coahuila (Carabaza, 2007). According to the latest 2010 census figures, the population of Saltillo is 725,123 inhabitants, of whom 599,012 were born in the state, 111,805 were born elsewhere and 2,745 are from another country and live in the city due to migration (Naal, 2013). (See Figure 1.2)

The census reveals that the female population outnumbers the male population, accounting for 50.4 percent, or 365,757 women, while men account for 49.6 percent, or 359,366. The number of married citizens is higher than the number of single citizens, as 311,033 people are married and 185,820 are single. According to the sociodemographic picture, only 2.2 percent are divorced and 3 percent are separated in terms of marital status. Regarding marital status, 84.9 percent of the population is married and 84.9 percent is single. Concerning religious faith, 84.9 percent of the population identifies as Roman Catholic (INEGI, 2010), a religion that condemns divorce and promotes marriage until death as one of its fundamental principles.

Regarding the field of education, at the higher education level, more men complete a bachelor's degree or other degrees, compared to women, with 52,959 men and 47,959 women, indicating that there are more male professionals (Naal, 2013). The above figure is congruent with an economically active population. In this sense, in the city, 73 percent of men are economically active in contrast to 35.4 percent of women who perform an activity that generates income, of whom 49.2 percent are engaged in household-related activities (INEGI, 2010).

The figures point to a society made up of a greater number of people from the city, mostly women, a high rate of male professionals, within a city where its inhabitants are mostly married, with the state ranking thirtieth nationally in terms of female-headed households (INEGI, 2012).

Some of the characteristics of Saltillo society fit with Díaz-Guerrero's (1982) analysis of the psychological structure of the Mexican family, especially in terms of the activities carried out by the two genders. According to the statistics, we observe a society where the provider is the man and the woman continues to be in charge of household-related activities. With regard to violence, figures show that 36.2 percent of married women suffered violence from their spouse, 85.2 percent of which was emotional, including threats, prohibitions and belittling; 55.2 percent was economic, where the partner complains about the wife spending money or does not provide for household expenses (ENDIREH, 2011).

Another interesting fact within Saltillo society, which is presented here for consideration, is again of a legal nature. The former governor Rubén Moreira presented an initiative regarding the State Civil Code, to repeal section IV of article 261 and articles 362 to 385; to add articles 362 to 375; and to reform section III of article 552 of code, in order to introduce the figure of divorce for no reason (Congress of the State of Coahuila, 2012). This occurred in 2013 when divorce for no reason was approved, and the term refers to the fact that either spouse may request a divorce before the judicial authority and express their wish not to remain within the marriage, without the requirement of indicating the reason for requesting it (CNDH, 2013).

This type of divorce is a reality in the state, and with this modification, the 21 existing causal factors that used to exist in the criminal legislation to carry out a divorce were eliminated; only the decision of one of the spouses to end the relationship and make the request before a judge is now necessary (Valdes, 2013). This type of procedure aims to speed up the dissolution of the marital bond and seeks to avoid further conflict and exhaustion for those who decide to legally separate (De Koster, 2013). These actions have a positive aspect in that they aim at lessening the damage that a separation process entails for a couple of individuals who are emotionally worn out by grief over the loss of a union.

In conclusion, the statistics reviewed show a society in which a rigid psychological structure predominates, as the male gender continues to have power in the economic and professional spheres. The female figure continues to be responsible for household activities, and in the religious aspect, the Roman Catholic faith predominates. The divorce rate, at least in Saltillo, shows low indicators, although it is perceived as a society in which reports from the civil registry show signs of gradual change that perhaps future generations will be able to adopt without so much resistance.

The belief in marriage is important, since it is a society that is mostly married, and the indicators of violence indicate that emotional violence continues to predominate, certainly, in lower percentages than the figures presented in the national indicators. However, this does not mean that the problem does not exist regarding the lack of factors favoring a culture of peace within marriage.

Same-sex marriage

In a society with old structures of rigid gender behavior, at least in terms of the economic aspect of the marriage relationship, there are flashes of contrast, in which the state has been a forerunner and promoter of legal same-sex marriage.

In 2007, the state of Coahuila amended its civil code and added in the sixth session article 195–1 regarding the civil pact of solidarity (Civil Code for the State of Coahuila de Zaragoza, 2008), which allows people of the same sex to share legal rights through a contract

(Zapata, 2013). Signs of evolution within a society have already been described above. In 2014, Coahuila became the second Mexican state to approve same-sex marriage, previously approved only by Mexico City, in the face of complaints from various opposition groups, such as the Roman Catholic Church, that legalization was intended to destroy the family. However, Coahuila was able to take the next step despite resistance from some groups (Rauters, 2014).

After the approval of same-sex marriage in Coahuila, 30,000 people marched against it, organized by a religious group, asking Congress to repeal the reforms (Fernández, 2014). These types of actions within the state result in a contrast between different types of thinking in Saltillo society. On the one hand, from a legal perspective, there is openness and an alternative is offered to different sexual preferences with the possibility of obtaining legal rights through marriage; however, there is at the same time religious resistance, which, as noted in the previous statistics, is that a large part of the inhabitants practice Catholicism, in which the power of beliefs regarding marriage continues to be reaffirmed.

In a system of ideas that only accepts what leaders have been proposing for years, without allowing those ideas to be questioned, and it is necessary to conduct research to determine the type of coexistence that is generated between people of the same sex and to discover whether or not there is a development of skills that could establish peaceful dynamics and not be violent, as the statistics show in hetero marriages.

Continuing with the discussion on the population under study, it is necessary to describe the object of study in its entirety. In this case, the individuals who voluntarily participated in the quantitative research have an interesting factor in common: they are men and women who belong to the generation known as "baby boomers". At present, it appears that no research has been carried out, at least at the local level, on this type of population that shows interesting characteristics.

Baby boomer generation

This section aims to describe the baby boomer generation, in order to understand specifically the population studied in the research, who belong to this generation. This section discusses the characteristics they share, the historical context in which they emerged and the psychological profile that distinguishes them.

Saltillo residents who were surveyed and interviewed for the study have in common that they belong to the same generation. The term "generation", as defined by Gilburg (2007, as cited in Chirinos, 2009), is an age group that shares a set of educational customs that make them distinguishable. This means that the group of subjects have in common their being born at a certain time in history, which makes them similar in terms of historical events and their contextual development. In this sense, López (2010) points out that the baby boomers are those born between 1946 and 1964.

This group of people have in common that they were born after the World War II; they are characterized by being idealistic and in need of making changes in the world; they are not satisfied with what they were given; and they are introverted, moralistic, conceited and self-confident (Chirinos, 2009). As they belong to a post-war era, they are considered to show a certain rebelliousness; they tend to revolutionize the schemes proposed by society, because they lived through the hippie movement; and in the workplace they are traditionalists, with rigid rules, vision and knowledge. Some of the representative figures of this generation are Bill Gates and Steve Jobs (Zamora, 2015).

For this generation, work represents a fixed point in life. The events that defined them were: prosperity, the beginning of television, and the civil rights and women's liberation movements; therefore, their personality reflects a positive attitude. They are optimistic, positive, open to change and traditionalists. They like to have achievements and want to have everything. Within their psychological profile, studies indicate that they are loyal, competitive and workaholics. In terms of family dynamics, men are usually the head of the family and women do the housework (Chirinos, 2009). Crampton and Hodge (2007, as cited in Shragay & Tziner, 2011) indicate that the various social changes they experienced caused them to be able to accept change with a positive attitude. It is perceived that through experiencing various social changes, including the hippie movements that advocated relationships based on peace and love, there may be some indication of these individuals opposing violence. This assumption, as well as the data that have been mentioned, may or may not be verified after having analyzed the results of the research.

Carrying out a study within a sector of the population such as Saltillo society, located in the eighth most peaceful state in Mexico, according to the Peace Index (2016), allows us to learn about specific positive behaviors that marriages with traditional and conservative structures have developed over a long period of union, and that have strengthened the culture of peace in their marriages.

Millennial generation

In contrast, the generation called millennials manages their situations differently than the baby boomers. Members of the millennial generation grew up in times of technological, social and cultural transformation that gave them characteristics that fostered new family schemes. This generation had to grow up in families where both parents participated in the workplace, or where their parents established new relationships and they had to learn to live with other siblings in a blended family (Vázquez-Gutiérrez & Cabello-Tijerina, 2018). According to Fernández Escárzaga and Vázquez Soto (2017), a number of quantitative and qualitative changes have been observed in the last recognized generation:

- Families are becoming smaller.
- The family dynamics described in the previous section, focused basically on the repetition of patterns inherited from earlier generations that took as a reference the paternal figure, the new education and formative and transmission environment have changed this new generation. For example, they are less attached to traditional gender roles; they delay parenting; they go online for help and information about raising their children; and they maintain a high consumption of technological items.

As you can see, socializing spaces in this generation are intimately related to the use of technologies, and these junctures should be used in the formation of attitudes and skills for the positive management of conflicts and to collaborate in the construction of a values-based culture (Vázquez-Gutiérrez & Cabello-Tijerina, 2018).

Reflection questions

1. What was the purpose of marriage in ancient times?
2. Is intimate partner violence a phenomenon exclusive to developing countries? Justify your answer.
3. Is violence against women exclusive to men? Justify your answer.
4. What are the side effects of violence within marriage?
5. How are human beings born violent? Justify your answer?
6. What are the positions of the different schools of thought on human violence?
7. What does the deficit theory propose?
8. What is conflict?
9. What is the psychological structure of the old Mexican family?
10. What is the baby boomer generation?

References

Abrego Franco, M. G. (2010). *La situacion de la educaciòn para la paz en Mèxico en la actualidad.* Obtenido de Espacios Públicos. www.redalyc.org/pdf/676/67613199010.pdf

Acevedo Velasco, V., & Restrepo de Giraldo, L. (2010). *Experiencias de parejas sobre vivir feliz en pareja.* Obtenido de Pensamiento Psicológico: www.redalyc.org/articulo.oa?id=80115648006

Albert, S. P. (2013). Naturaleza humana y conflicto: Un estudio desde la Filosofía para la Paz. *Eikasia, revista de Filosofía,* 107–16.

Alonso García, J. (2005). Prácticas educativas familiares y autoestima. Obtenido de Psicothema: www.psicothema.com/pdf/3067.pdf

Araque, F., & Rodríguez, X. (mayo-agosto de 2008). *Familias y discurso escolar.* Obtenido de Omnia: www.redalyc.org/pdf/737/73714203.pdf

Asamblea Genera. (4 de diciembre de 2006). *Asamblea General .* Obtenido de Naciones Unidas: https://documents-dds-ny.un.org/doc/UNDOC/GEN/N06/497/16/PDF/N0649716.pdf?OpenElement

Asamblea Legislativa del Distrito Federal. (17 de noviembre de 2013). *Urgen Erradicar Violencia en Noviazgo en DF.* Obtenido de www.aldf.gob.mx/comsoc-urgen-erradicar-violencia-noviazgo-df--15774.html

Barrio Maestre, J. (2001). *El marco sociocultural de la educación para la paz.* Obtenido de Educación y Educadores: www.redalyc.org/articulo.oa?id=83440403

Boletín UNAM-DGCS-403. (8 de junio de 2011). *Violencia en el Noviazgo Afecta a 76 por Ciento de las Parejas Mexicanas.* Obtenido de www.dgcs.unam.mx/boletin/bdboletin/2011_403.html

Burns, D. (2009). *Sentirse Bien en pareja. El secreto para hacer que las relaciones funcionen.* Barcelona: Paidos Iberica.
Cabello-Tijerina, P., & Vázquez-Gutiérrez, R. (2020). *Cultura de Paz.* Cuidad de México: Patria.
Cabello-Tijerina, P. A. (2021). *Tratado de justicia alternativa. Una guía de pacificación social.* Cuidad de México: Tirant Lo Blanch.
Cabello-Tijerina, P. A., & Vázquez-Gutiérrez, R. L. (2018). *Cultura y Educación para la Paz.* Cuidad de México: Tirant lo Blanch.
Calderón, C. P. (2009). Teoría de Conflictos de Johan Galtung. *Revista de paz y conflictos,* 60–81.
Carabaza González, J. (enero–abril de 2007). *El papel de la prensa en la construcción de las representaciones sobre la problemática ambiental en los habitantes de Saltillo, Coahuila.* Recuperado el 10 de abril de 2015, de Convergencia. Revista de Ciencias Sociales: www.redalyc.org/pdf/105/10504303.pdf
Chica Jiménez, M. (noviembre de 2007). *Del conflicto a la cultura de paz: Implicaciones.* Obtenido de Revista Iberoamericana de Educación: www.rie oei.org/deloslectores/1940Chica.pdf
Chirinos, N. (julio–diciembre de 2009). *Características generacionales y los valores. Su impacto en lo laboral.* Recuperado el 7 de noviembre de 2006, de Observatorio Laboral Revista Venezolana: www.redalyc.org/pdf/2190/219016846007.pdf
CNDH. (mayo de 2013). *Divorcio Incausado.* Recuperado el 20 de diciembre de 2014, de CNDH: www.cndh.org.mx/sites/all/fuentes/documentos/programas/ .../c.pdf
Codigo Civil para el estado de Coahuila de Zaragoza. (18 de enero de 2008). *Codigo Civil para el estado de Coahuila de Zaragoza.* Obtenido de Codigo Civil para el estado de Coahuila de Zaragoza: http://docs.mexico.justia.com.s3.amazonaws. com/estatales/coahuila/codigo-civil-para-el-estado-de-coahuila-de-zaragoza.pdf
Congreso del Estado de Coahuila. (6 de agosto de 2012). *Iniciativa de Decreto .* Recuperado el 1 de mayo de 2017, de Congreso del Estado de Coahuila: www. congresocoahuila.gob.mx/portal/wp-content/uploads/2014/11/20120806_Ejec_ 25.pdf
Correa, N. G. (2010). *Tolerancia a la Frustración .* Obtenido de Boletín del Grupo de Puericultura de la Universidad de Antioquia: www.udea.edu.co/portal/page/ portal/bibliotecaSedesDependencias/unidadesAcademicas/FacultadMedicina/ BilbiotecaDiseno/Archivos/PublicacionesMedios/BoletinPrincipioActivo/cri anza_humanizada_117.pdf
Cruz Zuluaga, M. (20 de abril de 2013). *La programación neurolingüística en el proceso de enseñanza-aprendizaje.* Obtenido de Escenarios: Empresa y Territorio: http://investigaciones.esumer.edu.co/revista/index.php/revista/article/ view/47/37
De Koster, L. (7 de febrero de 2013). *Habrá sana separación con divorcio incausado.* Recuperado el 13 de abril de 2015, de Zócalo Saltillo: www.zocalo.com.mx/secc ion/articulo/habra-sana-separacion-con-divorcio-incausado-1360216234
De Ocáriz, G. U., & Burgués, L. P. (2014). Hacia una transformación de los conflictos motores en Educación Física. *Cultura, ciencia y deporte,* 43–55.
Diario Oficial de la Federación. (30 de abril de 2014). *Secretaría de Gobernación.* Obtenido de Programa Integral para Prevenir, Atender, Sancionar y Erradicar la

Violencia contra las Mujeres 2014–2018: www.dof.gob.mx/nota_detalle.php?cod igo=5343064&fecha=30/04/2014

Diaz-Guerrero, R. (1982). *Psicologia del mexicano: descubrimiento de la etnopsicología.* Trillas.

Díaz-Martínez, A. (2003). *Violencia intrafamiliar.* Obtenido de Gaceta Médica de México: www.medigraphic.com/pdfs/gaceta/gm-2003/gm034gI.pdf

DIF Nacional. (2009). *Buen Trato.* Recuperado el 20 de marzo de 2015, de DIF Nacional: http://sn.dif.gob.mx/transparencia/transparencia-focalizada/buen-trato/

El Universal. (2 de julio de 2013). *Mèxico, Pais con mas estres laboral.* Obtenido de www.eluniversal.com.mx/ciencia/2013/mexico-pais-mas-estres-laboral-78744.html

Encuestas Nacionales sobre la Dinámica de las Relaciones en los Hogares. (2011). *Violencia de Gènero. Violencia contra mujeres.* Obtenido de Sistema de Indicadores de Género: http://estadistica.inmujeres.gob.mx/formas/tarjetas/Violencia_2011.pdf

ENDIREH. (2011). *Estadisticas a propósito del 14 de febrero, matrimonios y divorcios en México: Datos de Coahuila.* Recuperado el 13 de noviembre de 2014, de INEGI: www.inegi.org.mx/inegi/contenidos/.../estadisticas/.../matrimoni os5.pdf

Fernández, H. (28 de septiembre de 2014). *Marchan miles contra uniones gay en Saltillo.* Recuperado el 13 de abril de 2015, de El Universal: www.eluniversal.com.mx/estados/2014/marchan-miles-contra-matrimonios-gay-saltillo-1041884.html

Fernández Escárzaga, J., & Vázquez Soto, M. (2017). La evolución de la familia y los estilo de educación. *Revista Electrónica sobre Cuerpos Académicos y Grupos de Investigación, 4*(8).

Fisas, V. (1998). *Cultura de paz y gestión de conflictos.* Barcelona: Icaria/NESCO. Obtenido de (capítulo XI del libro "Cultura de paz y gestión de conflictos".

Fuquen Alvarado, M. E. (2003). Los conflictos y las formas alternativas de resolución. *Tabula Rasa, 1,* 265–78.

Formet, E. (2021). *El matrimonio.* Obtenido de InfoCatolica: www.infocatolica.com/blog/sapientia.php/2107151017-cx-el-matrimonio

Galtung, J. (20 de septiembre de 2010). *"Me impresiona la idea de unos Estados Unidos de Latinoamérica.* Recuperado el 3 de marzo de 2014, de Deutsche Welle: Conferencia en el GIGA de Hamburgo el 17 de septiembre sobre tendencias de desarrollo del orden mundial: www.dw.de/johan-galtung-me-imp resiona-la-idea-de-unos-estados-unidos-de-latinoam%C3%A9rica/a-6021716-1

Goleman, D. (1995). *La Iinteligencia Emocional.* Buenos Aires: Vergara.

Gómez B., G. (diciembre de 2008). *Affectio Societatis.* Obtenido de Freud: Enfermedades nerviosas, angustia y estres: http://aprendeenlinea.udea.edu.co/revistas/index.php/affectiosocietatis/issue/view/572

Gorjón Gómez, F. J., & Sáenz López, K. A. (2009). *Mètodos Alternos de Soluciòn de Controversias.* D.F.: Patria.

Hueso García, V. (2000). *Johan Galtung La transformación de los conflictos por medios pacíficos.* Obtenido de Cuadernos de estrategia: http://dialnet.unirioja.es/servlet/articulo?codigo=595158

Índice de Paz México 2016 vía el Instituto para la Economía y la Paz. (2016). *Índice de Paz México 2016 vía el Instituto para la Economía y la Paz* . Recuperado el 15 de noviembre de 2016, de IMCO: http://imco.org.mx/seguridad/indice-de-paz-mexico-2016-via-el-instituto-para-la-economia-y-la-paz/

INEGI. (2010). *Panorama sociodemográfico de Coahuila de Zaragoza.* Recuperado el 10 de abril de 2015, de INEGI: www.inegi.org.mx/prod_serv/contenidos/espanol/bvinegi/productos/censos/poblacion/2010/panora_socio/coah/Panorama_Coah.pdf

INEGI. (diciembre de 2012). *Perspectiva estadística de Coahuila de Zaragoza* . Recuperado el 10 de abril de 2015, de INEGI: www.inegi.org.mx/prod_serv/contenidos/espanol/bvinegi/productos/integracion/estd_perspect/coah/Pers-coa.pdf

INEGI. (23 de Noviembre de 2021). *Comunicados de prensa. INEGI.* Obtenido de INEGI: www.inegi.org.mx/contenidos/saladeprensa/aproposito/2021/EAP_Elimviolmujer21.pdf

Jimenez, Bautista, F. (2014). Paz neutra: Una ilustración del concepto. *Revista de Paz y Conrictos*, 19–52.

Labrador, C. (2000). *Educación para la Paz y Cultura de Paz en Documentos Internacionales.* Obtenido de Contextos Educativos: http://dialnet.unirioja.es/descarga/articulo/201070.pdf

Laca Arocena, F. (2006). *Cultura de paz y psicología del conflicto.* Obtenido de Estudios sobre las Culturas Contemporaneas: www.redalyc.org/articulo.oa?id=31602404

Lara García, C. (7 de mayo de 2014). Mèxico, Pais con mayor violencia de pareja. *El Universal*, págs. www.eluniversal.com.mx/periodismo-datos/2014/mexico-mayor-violencia-pareja-ocde-88181.html.

Loinaz, I., Echeburúa, E., & Torrubia, R. (2010). *Tipología de agresores contra la pareja en prisión.* Obtenido de Psicothema: www.unioviedo.net/reunido/index.php/PST/article/view/9008/8872

López Colás, J. (2010). *Reseña de "Immigrants and Boomers: Forging a New Social Contract for the Future of America" de Dowell Myers.* Recuperado el 11 de noviembre de 2016, de Reis. Revista Española de Investigaciones Sociológicas: www.redalyc.org/pdf/997/99717150010.pdf

López Monroy, J. (1991). *Concepto de matrimonio.* Recuperado el 1 de mayo de 2017, de Revista de derecho privado: https://revistas-colaboracion.juridicas.unam.mx/index.php/rev-derecho-privado/article/view/20025/17968

Matsuura, K. (enero de 2004). *Diálogo entre las civilizaciones.* Obtenido de UNESCO: https://es.unesco.org/courier/enero-2004

Melgar, I., & Hernández, L. (18 de mayo de 2014). *La pobreza está anclada en México.* Recuperado el 7 de abril de 2015, de Excelsior: www.excelsior.com.mx/nacional/2014/05/18/959942

Miller, L., Dell Smith, A., & Rothstein, L. (1994). *Los Distintos tipos de estrés.* Recuperado el 27 de mayo de 2015, de American Psychological Association: www.apa.org/centrodeapoyo/tipos.aspx

Mirón Pérez, M. (2014). La paz en femenino género, mito y valores de paz en grecia antigua. En F. Muñoz, & B. Molina Rueda, *Virtudes clásicas para la paz* (pág. 75). Granada: Universidad de Granada.

Montero-Medina, D., Bolivar-Guayacundo, M., Aguirre-Encalada, L., & Moreno-Estupiñan, A. (2020). *Violencia intrafamiliar en el marco de la emergencia sanitaria por el COVID-19*. Obtenido de Revista CienciAmerica: https://dialnet.uniri oja.es/servlet/articulo?codigo=7746453

Moreno Angel, L., Hernández, J., & García Leal, O. (2000). *Un test informatizado para la evaluación de la Tolerancia a la frustración*. Obtenido de Anales de Psicologia: http://digitum.um.es/xmlui/bitstream/10201/7956/1/Un%20test%20in formatizado%20para%20la%20evaluacion%20de%20la.pdf

Múnera, M. M. (9 de enero de 2021). Obreros de Hiram Abiff: Los conflictos. Obtenido de En el Nacional: www.elnacional.com/opinion/obreros-de-hiram-abiff-los-conflictos/

Muñoz, A. (2005). *Baja Tolerancia a la Frustación*. Recuperado el 12 de febrero de 2015, de Centro de Atención Terapeútica de Barcelona: www.cat-barcelona.com/pdf/filosofia/BTF.pdf

Muñoz, F., & Molina Rueda, B. (2010). *Una Cultura de Paz compleja y conflictiva. La búsqueda de equilibrios dinámicos*. Obtenido de Revista de Paz y Conflictos: www.dh.iteso.mx/textos1/PAZ_Compleja_y_Conflictiva_Mu%C3%B1oz_Molina.pdf

Naal, S. (25 de julio de 2013). *Saltillo en números*. Recuperado el 10 de abril de 2015, de Periodico Vanguardia: www.vanguardia.com.mx/saltilloennumeros-1793843.html

Naciones Unidas. (2005). *Informe de la Comisión de Consolidación de la Paz; Informe del Secretario General sobre el Fondo para la Consolidación de la Paz: Debate conjunto*. Obtenido de Naciones Unidas: www.un.org/es/ga/62/plenary/peacebuil ding_commission/bkg.shtml

Naciones Unidas. (2009). *Repertorio de la práctica del Consejo de Seguridad*. New York: Naciones Unidas.

Naciones Unidas. (2010). *Año Internacional de acercamiento a las culturas*. Obtenido de Naciones Unidas: www.un.org/es/events/iyrc2010/

Naciones Unidas. (2022). *Objetivos de Desarrollo Sostenible*. Obtenido de Naciones Unidas: www.un.org/sustainabledevelopment/es/2015/09/la-asamblea-general-adopta-la-agenda-2030-para-el-desarrollo-sostenible/

Niccolo & Maffeo. (2007). *Mapa de Saltillo*. Recuperado el 17 de mayo de 2016, de Niccolo & Maffeo: www.niccolomaffeo.es/mexicorepublica/mapas/capitales/saltillo.htm

Nicólas Guardiola, J. J. (agosto–diciembre de 2011). *¿Qué es la Tolerancia?* Obtenido de Archivos de Criminología, criminalistica y Seguridad Privada: file:///C:/Users/Toshiba/Downloads/Dialnet-QueEsLaTolerancia-4016230.pdf

Oliva Delgado, A., Antolín Suárez, L., Pertegal Vega, M. Á., Ríos Bermúdez, M., Parra Jiménez, Á., & Hernándo Gómez, Á. (2011). *Instrumentos para evaluar el desarrollo positivo adolescente y los activos familiares, escolares y comunitarios que lo promueven*. Recuperado el 14 de marzo de 2015, de Andalucía Consejería de Salud: http://personal.us.es/oliva/INSTRUMENTOS_DESARROLLO%20P OSITIVO.pdf

Organización Mundial de la Salud. (2012). Obtenido de Plan de Acción de la Campaña Mundial de Prevención de la Violencia 2012: www.who.int/violence_in jury_prevention/violence/global_campaign/actionplan/es/

Organización Mundial de la Salud. (27 de abril de 2020). Organización Mundial de la Salud . Obtenido de COVID-19: cronología de la actuación de la OMS: www.who.int/es/news/item/27-04-2020-who-timeline---covid-19

Osorio García, S. (julio–diciembre de 2012). Conflicto, Violencia y Paz: Un acercamiento científico, filosófico y bioético. Obtenido de Revista Latinoamericana de Bioética: www.redalyc.org/pdf/1270/127025833006.pdf

Pacrez, D. T. (15 de junio de 2008). *CNN EXPANSIÓN*. Obtenido de Alternativas Pacíficas con las mujeres: www.cnnexpansion.com/emprendedores/2008/06/15/la-otra-mejilla

Pantelides, E., & Manzelli, H. (julio–septiembre de 2005). *Papeles de Población*. Obtenido de Violencia en la pareja. Evidencias a partir de encuestas a hombres centroamericanos: www.redalyc.org/pdf/112/11204510.pdf

Pérez Contreras, M. d. (mayo–agosto de 1999). *La violencia Intrafamiliar*. Obtenido de Boletin Mexicano de Derecho Comparado: www.juridicas.unam.mx/publica/rev/boletin/cont/95/art/art9.htm#N4

Polaino-Lorente, A., & Martínez Cano, P. (2002). *La comunicación en la pareja, errores psicologicos más comunes*. Madrid: Ediciones Rialp.

Pozos Gutiérrez, J., Rivera Aragón, S., Reidl Martínez, L., & Vargas Núñez, B. (enero–junio de 2013). *Felicidad General y Felicidad en la pareja: diferencias por sexo y estado civil*. Obtenido de Enseñanza e Investigación en Psicología: www.redalyc.org/articulo.oa?id=29228948005

Proceso. (10 de octubre de 2006). *Violencia generalizada contra mujeres en el mundo, revela la OMS*. Obtenido de www.proceso.com.mx/?p=222018

Programa Conjunto por una Cultura de Paz. (12 de 7 de 2012). *Programa Conjunto por una Cultura de Paz*. Obtenido de http://culturadepaz.org.mx/sitio/

Ramírez Solórzano, M. (2013). *Hombres Violentos, Un estudio Antropologico de la vioencia masculina en la relación de pareja en el ambito familiar*. Madrid: Plaza y Valdes.

Rauters. (2 de septiembre de 2014). *Coahuila aprueba el matrimonio entre parejas del mismo sexo*. Recuperado el 13 de abril de 2015, de CNN: http://mexico.cnn.com/nacional/2014/09/02/coahuila-aprueba-el-matrimonio-entre-parejas-del-mismo-sexo

Redacción Nacional Conecta. (28 de diciembre de 2021). 2021 El segundo año de la pandemia y las noticias que marcaron. Obtenido de Conecta. Tecnológico de Monterrey: https://tec.mx/es/noticias/nacional/institucion/2021-el-segundo-ano-de-pandemia-y-las-noticias-que-lo-marcaron

Redorta, J. (2006). *Cómo analizar los conflictos: la tipologia de conflictos como herramienta de mediación*. Barcelona: PAIDOS IBERICA.

Redorta, J. (2014). *Como actuar ante un conflicto. 50 reglas útiles de fácil uso*. Cordova: Almuzara.

Redorta, J., Obiols, M., & Bisquerra, R. (2006). *Emoción y Conflicto*. Barcelona: Paidós Ibérica.

Resolución de la Asamblea General. (11 de abril de 2000). *El Año Internacional para el Diálogo entre las Civilizaciones*. Obtenido de Incolturación: http://inculturacion.net/phocadownload/Autores_invitados/Sanchez,_Para_el_dialogo_entre_civilizaciones.pdf

Resolución de la Asamblea General. (2006). Decenio Internacional de una culuta de paz y no violencia para los niños del mundo. Obtenido de: https://documents-dds-ny.un.org/doc/UNDOC/GEN/N06/497/16/PDF/N0649716.pdf?Open Element

Rivera-Rivera, L., Allen, B., Rodríguez-Ortega, G., Chávez-Ayala, R., & Lazcano-Ponce, E. (2006). *Violencia durante el noviazgo, depresión y conductas de riesgo en estudiantes femeninas 12–24 años.* Recuperado el 6 de abril de 2015, de Salud Pública de México: http://scielo.unam.mx/scielo.php?pid=S0036-36342006000800009&script=sci_arttext

Rivera Salazar, J., Murillo Villa, J., & Sierra Rubio, M. (enero–junio de 2007). *Enseñanza e Investigación en Psicología.* Obtenido de El concepto de neurosis de William Cullen como revolución científica: www.redalyc.org/pdf/292/29212111.pdf

Rodriguez, D. J. (2005). *El matrimonio cristiano en San Agustin.* Obtenido de Anuario Jurídico y Económico Escurialense: https://dialnet.unirioja.es/servlet/articulo?codigo=1142994

Rojas Donat, L. (2005). *Para una historia del matrimonio occidental. La sociedad romano-germánica. Siglos VI-XI.* Recuperado el 25 de marzo de 2014, de Theoria: www.redalyc.org/articuloBasic.oa?id=29900106

Rosenberg, M. B. (2006). *Comunicaciòn no violenta, un lenguaje de vida.* Buenos Aires: Fusión gran Aldea.

Ross, G. G., Cagnoni, A., Giser, E., Luciano, J., Cortés, L., Lerose, C., ... Dalbherg, P. (2013). *Encuesta sobre satisfacción laboral de los médicos de un Hospital Público.* Recuperado el 21 de marzo de 2015, de Intra Med: http://journal.intramed.net/index.php/Intramed_Journal/article/view/207

Saénz, G. C. (21 de febrero de 2021). Línea de tiempo COVID-19'; a un año del primer caso en México. Obtenido de Capital 21: www.capital21.cdmx.gob.mx/noticias/?p=12574

Sanmartín, J. (2011). Conceptos y tipos de violencia. En J. Sanmartín Espluges, R. Gutiérrez Lombardo, J. Martínez Contreras, & J. Vera Cortés, *Reflexiones sobre la Violencia* (págs. 11–33). Ciudad de México: Siglo XXI Editores.

Save the Children. (febrero de 2022). *En 2022, continua la grave violencia contra niños y niñas en México.* Obtenido de Debate: www.debate.com.mx/politica/En-2022-continua-la-grave-violencia-contra-ninos-y-ninas-en-Mexico--20220209-0037.html

Secretaría de Seguridad Pública. (mayo de 2010). *Maltrato y Abuso Infantil en Mèxico: Factor de Riezgo en la comisiòn de Delitos.* Obtenido de Secretarìa de Seguridad Pùblica: www.ssp.gob.mx/portalWebApp/ShowBinary?nodeId=/BEA%20Repository/1214170//archivo

Secretariado Ejecutivo del Sistema Nacional de Seguridad Pública. (21 de diciembre de 2021). Violación y Violencia Familiar los delitos que más aumentaron en el 2021. Obtenido de Expansión Política: https://politica.expansion.mx/mexico/2021/12/21/los-delitos-que-mas-aumentaron-en-2021-mexico

Shragay, D., & Tziner, A. (agosto de 2011). *The Generational Effect on the Relationship between Job Involvement, Work Satisfaction, and Organizational Citizenship Behavior.* Recuperado el 9 de noviembre de 2016, de Revista de

Psicología del Trabajo y de las Organizaciones: www.redalyc.org/pdf/2313/23132
2142006.pdf

Sistema de Naciones Unidas en México. (2010). *La ONU en México*. Obtenido de www.onu.org.mx/proyectos.html

Sistema Estatal para el Desarrollo de la Familia. (2011). *Estadísticas de Menores Maltratados del 2009 al 2011 DIF*. Obtenido de Fundación en Pantalla contra la violencia Infantil: www.fundacionenpantalla.org/estadisticas/pdf/DIF_%20ESTADISTICAS_MENORES_MALTRATADOS_DEL_2009_AL_2 011.pdf

Sistema Nacional de Seguridad Pública. (2020). En 2020, cada hora hubo 25 denuncias por violencia familiar. Obtenido de Animal Político: www.animalpolitico.com/2021/01/2020-cada-hora-hubo-25-denuncias-violencia-familiar/

Sociedades Bíblicas. (2021). *El matrimonio de acuerdo a la biblia*. Obtenido de Vive la Biblia: https://vivelabiblia.com/el-matrimonio-de-acuerdo-a-la-biblia/

Stenou, K. (2002). *Declaración Universal sobre la Diversidad Cultural: una visión, una plataforma conceptual, un semillero de ideas, un paradigma nuevo*. Obtenido de UNESCO: https://unesdoc.unesco.org/ark:/48223/pf0000127162_spa

Tironi, E. (mayo de 1989). *¿Pobreza = Frustración = Violencia? Crítica Empírica a un mito recurrente*. Obtenido de Kellogg Institute for International Studies: http://kellogg.nd.edu/publications/workingpapers/WPS/123.pdf

UN Department of Public Information. (noviembre de 2009). *Violencia contra las mujeres*. Obtenido de www.un.org/es/events/endviolenceday/pdfs/unite_the_situation_sp.pdf

UNESCO. (2013). *International Decade for the Rapprochement of Cultures (2013-2022)*. Obtenido de https://en.unesco.org/decade-rapprochement-cultures/milestones

UNESCO. (23 de octubre de 2014). *UNESCO Quito participa en el "II Encuentro Andino sobre Cultura de Paz - El rol de la Educación para Todos"*. Recuperado el 9 de marzo de 2015, de UNESCO: www.unesco.org/new/es/media-services/single-view/news/unesco_quito_participa_en_el_ii_encuentro_andino_sobre_cultura_de_paz_el_rol_de_la_educacion_para_todos/#.VP4kHnyG91Y

UNESCO. (2016). *Hoja de ruta, el acercamiento a las culturas*. Obtenido de UNESCO: https://unesdoc.unesco.org/ark:/48223/pf0000244334_spa

UNICEF. (2009). *La infancia*. Recuperado el 18 de marzo de 2015, de UNICEF México: www.unicef.org/mexico/spanish/ninos.html

United Nations. (2010). *Año Internacional de Acercamiento a las culturas*. Obtenido de: www.un.org/es/events/iyrc2010/background.shtml

United Nations. (2022). *Objetivos de Desarrollo Sostenible*. Obtenido de Naciones Unidas: www.un.org/sustainabledevelopment/es/2015/09/la-asamblea-general-adopta-la-agenda-2030-para-el-desarrollo-sostenible/

Valdes, D. (2 de marzo de 2013). *Divorcio incausado, una realidad en Coahuila*. Recuperado el 13 de abril de 2015, de El Diario de Coahuila: www.eldiariodecoahuila.com.mx/notas/2013/3/2/divorcio-incausado-realidad-coahuila-345914.asp

Vázquez-Gutiérrez, R. L., & Cabello-Tijerina, P. A. (2018). Gestión Pacífica de Conflictos en la Generación Millennial. En A. Sánchez, & P. López, *La solución alternativa de conflictos en los nuevos modelos de familia* (págs. 324–41). Pamplona: Aranzadi.

Villa Hernández, F. (30 de septiembre de 2007). *Psiquiatria y personalidad del mexicano.* Recuperado el 9 de abril de 2015, de Siglo de Torreón: www.elsiglodetorreon.com.mx/noticia/300812.psiquiatria-personalidad-del-mexicano.html

Zambrano Villalba, C. (2021). *Revisión sitemática: Violencia intrafamiliar en tiempos de confinamiento por COVID 19.* Obtenido de Perspectivas metodológicas: http://revistas.unla.edu.ar/epistemologia/article/view/3605

Zamora Rivera, L. (9 de abril de 2015). *¿Dónde están los baby boomers?* Recuperado el 25 de octubre de 2016, de Forbes México: www.forbes.com.mx/donde-estan-los-baby-boomers/

Zapata, B. (23 de diciembre de 2013). *2013, un año de avances para el matrimonio gay en México.* Recuperado el 13 de abril de 2015, de CNN México: http://mexico.cnn.com/nacional/2013/12/26/2013-un-ano-de-avances-para-el-matrimonio-gay-en-mexico

Chapter 2

Skill 1
Assertive language

The beginning of language

From birth, human beings find different ways of communicating, in their first months through crying and movements, as they grow physically, their communication skills change: from babbling to understanding that they can communicate their needs through speech, through language. According to studies carried out by paleoanthropologists (scientists specializing in ancient humans), speech, defined as the ability to pronounce words using the vocal cords with refined movements of the tongue, lips and nasal cavities, arrived with the appearance of Cro-Magnon man, this being the closest antecedent to the beginnings of language (Defleur et al., 2005).

Research reveals that 30,000 years ago, the ability to speak was well developed and that groups of humans in different parts of the world could talk to each other, tell stories, teach their children and generally communicate with speech as much as they do today, using a standardized vocabulary, with rules of pronunciation, syntax and grammar. What is unknown is the initial type of language; it is only known that it was spread and modified (Defleur et al., 2005).

According to the aforementioned studies, the existence of language as a form of communication is known from thousands of years ago. The interesting thing about this communication structure that Cro-Magnon man maintained is, if there was violent verbal communication or not since then, at what point in his evolution did man trigger this type of verbal violence, and more specifically, within marriage? Has it always existed since ancient humans?

DOI: 10.4324/9781003207023-3

Linguistics, the science of language

Research on language began more than 20 centuries ago by Greek rhetoricians and philosophers. It could be said that until the nineteenth century, language had never been studied in its true function; linguistics was an art before it became a science. At that time there were legitimate concerns, but these were foreign to the disinterested study of the true nature of language (Bally, 1977). According to Bally, modernity presents a better picture by considering language as a service of life, not the life of a few but the life of all, and in all its manifestations: its function is biological and social.

For some authors, the definition of language consists of the body of signs—usually words—and systems that are used in common messages by people who belong to the same linguistic community, referred to as the group of people who speak the same language (Verderber & Verderbe, 2005). For its part, the Royal Spanish Academy (2011) states that it is the set of articulated sounds with which man expresses what he thinks or feels. Jean Piaget (n.d., as cited in Silva, 2006) refers to the logical expressions of thought, pointing out that language is not necessarily thought but the coordination of interindividual actions, constituted by a system of conventional arbitrary signs.

But what is it really that we communicate—a thought, a feeling, an idea? Is it the existence of thoughts, ideas or needs that have not been clarified and reflected upon that produce violence in interpersonal communication? Piaget, from his perspective, points to the coordination of actions by signs that go against reason. An answer to the question above can be given if an analogy is made with the lack of connection between sounds and actions due to these opposing signs. Language, while sometimes used inappropriately and negatively to achieve the subjugation of another person and to promote power and gender inequality, also has a number of positive purposes. Authors such as Verderber and Verderbe (2005) point to a number of uses to which language is put:

- To designate, classify, define and limit; to differentiate something from something else.

- To evaluate: language conveys positive or negative attitudes toward individuals.
- To discuss things outside our immediate experience: to refer to past and future events, as well as to talk about absent people or things.
- To speak the language itself: to discuss the way someone elaborated a sentence or a better construction of ideas.

As mentioned before, language is used for different purposes, to describe, to differentiate, to discuss different ideas about a matter or event. The interpersonal language used by the couple within marriage is one of the central topics on which the science of communication conducts studies. In order to understand the issue of the couple, it is necessary to inquire about the origin of all being: the family.

The family language

It is difficult for people to remember how they learned to speak. It is a process that comes naturally to human beings, who completely forget the external influence exerted on them. It is amusing that in adult life, sometimes the intonation, vocabulary, idioms and even jokes a person makes are similar to those of the immediate family. Some authors observe that language has been learned by ear, that auditory and motor images have been deposited there, that all language's words and turns of phrase, even intonations of voice are in their smallest details, linked to thought (Bally, 1977). Bally mentions that in childhood, when language is learned, the child is a sensitive and imaginary being, and thought, without being exclusively attached to material objects, is added to practical life, so the child is is moved by the impulses of needs and desires and is oriented toward action.

According to the above, it could be said that the most vulnerable stage in the human being is childhood, a period in which information is assimilated without filters and will become a baggage of thoughts that will be expressed through words. It is essential that in the process of growth, the infant be surrounded by people who use appropriate, harmonious language, free of violence, because that is what his ear will learn and therefore repeat. For Bally (1977), language is transmitted by a social inheritance, against which the child is incapable of reacting as it is given; it is necessary to take it as it is and count on it. By convention, it is called the language of conversation or spoken language, although it can also be written. When its characters are discussed, the family language is mentioned, but this appellation condemns it rather than defines it. Based on Bally's thoughts, it is interpreted that perhaps the lack of components that favor a peaceful coexistence within marriage, at least in the aspect of oral communication, is a Mexican social inheritance that the population innately adopts in order to continue with patterns of emotional violence.

Language as a reflection of society

Given the problem of emotional violence in marriages that manifests itself through oral communication, what do statistics on the use of violent language within the first social cell of marriage reflect about a society? Trying to answer this question can possibly reflect a violent society and culture. Sociolinguists have used the idea of variety in language to reach four conclusions about the relationship between languages and the societies that speak or write them. These points may seem obvious enough when formulated in a simple or straightforward way, but they have not, at least so far, been fully integrated into the practice of social historians, for (Burke, 2001):

- Different social groups use different varieties of the language.
- The same individuals use different varieties of the language in different situations.
- Language reflects the society or culture in which it is used.
- Language shapes the society in which it is used.

By focusing on the conclusion that language reflects the society or culture in which it is used, Burke addresses first that an individual's accent, vocabulary and general style of speech reveal for anyone with a trained ear much about the individual's position in society.

Second, linguistic forms, their variations and changes, tell us something about the nature of the whole of social relations in a given culture. First, the characteristics of accent, vocabulary and style of emotional violence manifested by shouting, insults, threats, jealousy, humiliation, blackmail, emotional neglect, intimidation and indifference should be reviewed (Xbalanqué, 2012). According to the nature of social relationships, at least half of the married population in Mexico are in marriages of an emotionally violent nature, lacking values and components that are conducive to another form of speech.

The development of certain social dialects such as the languages of a profession or a trade, for example, the language of law, of the army and so on, must be explained not only in a utilitarian way, that is, as the creation of technical terms for practical purposes, but also in a symbolic way, as the expression of a group's growing consciousness and growing sense of the distance separating it from the rest of society (Burke, 2001). The creation of technical terms for practical purposes mentioned by Burke opens up the suggestion to use a new style of oral communication between people. The importance of speech in developing a new kind of awareness to find new ways of solving conflicts, without involving verbal emotional violence between two people.

Interpersonal oral communication

Maldonado Willman (1998) defines oral communication, also called interindividual, as taking place directly between two or more people, who are physically close, with an immediate response. He also conceptualizes interpersonal communication as an interaction situation, in which an individual—the communicator—in a face-to-face context transmits stimuli to modify the behavior of other individuals. According to the Maldonado Willman, if communication occurs in such a way that each participant can see the face of the other at a close distance, this is interpersonal communication, but it also occurs when there is a barrier such as a window, a lamp and so on. Therefore, he points out a series of five characteristics of this type of communication:

1. Perceptual participation of two or more persons.
2. A single focus of visual cognitive attention.
3. Interaction occurs through an exchange of messages in which the participants reciprocally offer each other some signals.
4. Interaction is face-to-face and all senses can be engaged.
5. A largely unstructured interpersonal context; that is, the frequency, form or content of the message is governed by few rules.

According to studies in the *Manual of Oral Communication*, the study of interpersonal communication is concerned with investigating social situations where people interact through the reciprocal exchange of verbal or nonverbal signals. For Rosenberg (2006), interpersonal communication presents other types of characteristics, which he identifies as the elements of observation; feeling and need; and the necessity for verbal communication to be nonviolent, in which one intervenes by not speaking critically or blaming the other, and acting in a way that dialogue gives rise to the creation of understanding and compassion.

The creation of certain elements by the aforementioned authors that function to achieve efficient oral communication requires the knowledge and introspection of the individual in order to be objective in the real requirements and to be able to express them with an objective intention. A type of education that favors the development of feelings of compassion and understanding with the other is perceived as necessary; this type of behavior requires training from infancy, a stage in which the child assimilates directly what he or she hears and then expresses it through words. These types of educational tools can be focused on developing peaceful intentions through paralinguistic codes that favor a communication environment free of violence.

A glance at paralinguistic codes

Following the structure of communication based on nonviolence, as a fundamental principle of the culture of peace, the appropriate use of paralinguistic codes is proposed as a suitable means for the creation of atmospheres that facilitate a dialogue in which understanding, comprehension and nonviolence are the predominant elements.

Paralinguistic means the modality of nonverbal communication that indicates how things are said: vocally, phonically, sonorously, and is expressed by the quality of voice and various types of vocalizations or the absence of these. Fernando Poyatos explains the details of these characteristics (Aguila, 2010) in the following:

a) Voice quality: refers to nonverbal traits such as pitch, timbre, volume, rhythm.
b) Differentiators: emotional sounds or reactions such as laughing, crying, snoring, coughing, burping, and so forth.
c) Quasi-lexical or alternating paralinguistic elements: interjections—exclamatory utterances, onomatopoeia—words that have a sound similar to their meaning—and sound emissions with a name, but without spelling.
d) The absence of sounds: these are pauses and silences.

For García (2008), communication is an active process that requires encoding, transmitting and decoding the message, where paralinguistic codes such as intonation, emphasis, speed of speech and pauses cover the speech, indicating what is the attitude and intonation of the communicator. Knowing the codes would encourage their regulation, which could produce a positive intention within the communication process. In the past, four main elements were recognized: the sender, message, receiver and feedback. Nowadays, authors such as Fajardo Uribe (2009) consider that there are eight elements: sender, receiver, code, intention of the speaker, message, channel, the context, objectives of the communication. The aim of communication and the intention of the speaker, says Fajardo Uribe, are aspects of pragmatic and cognitive theory that should be included in the analysis of verbal communication.

Within the codes, tone is the most complex. It can indicate emotions as well as express the importance given to the information being expressed. The pace of speech changes according to the emotion of the person speaking, and the confidence he or she has with the content he or she is handling (García, 2008). García points out that there is a tendency to speak quickly when there is a high level of stimulation. When the information is really known, or when there is a conviction that the receiver is understanding, pauses are used to make a distinction of important information.

The words that are selected, the way sentences are structured and the intonation reflect something beyond the words, so the receiver has to analyze and measure the intention to produce a response. The use of language creates power interests, desires and emotions. Its aim is to shape, change and construct the world that is represented through words, structures and extra-linguistic mechanisms (Fajardo, 2009).

Within a socio-pragmatic study, Bravo (2008, as cited in Escamilla & Vega, 2012) proposes linguistic analysis based on a series of categories: act, strategy and resource. The act is the purpose of communication; the strategy consists of softening a self-criticism; the resources used are verbal, nonverbal and paraverbal. These three resources combined produce an alleviating effect; they seek to attenuate a negative effect on the speaker's image. This type of deeper analysis through the categories indicated by Bravo provides a method by which people can maneuver their communication, obtaining the results they are looking for with the activation of the appropriate intonation, volume and rhythm of voice, since according to Bravo, the paraverbal interpretation codes are more immediate and automatic than the verbal ones.

Gender differences in oral communication

Why is the matter of interpersonal communication within marriage complex? The negative social inheritance that is reproduced, and how it was acquired during childhood were addressed above as some of the precedents that could answer this question; however, there is still a fundamental aspect that has not yet been addressed, which is the gender characteristics that distinguish man and woman.

In investigations of the differences in communication between genders, authors such as Mulac refer to two disagreements about language use between men and women, both of which seem to be strongly supported (Verderber & Verderbe, 2005).

1. Females tend to use more reinforcers and more boundaries than males. Reinforcers are words that modify other words and serve to strengthen the idea represented by the original word.
2. Women ask questions more often than men. They tend to use questions to elicit more information, elaborate and determine how others feel about the information.

A study carried out by Locke (2011), a researcher in gender linguistics, refers to the way men communicate with other men and points out that conversation becomes a duel of rivals in which status and sex are the matters of greatest interest. In the case of women, in contrast, communication is like a harmonious verbal duet in which more private thoughts and feelings are shared. For Lakkof (1990, as cited in Fajardo, 2009), the use of language is marked by some gender differences, which are the following:

- The tone of voice used by women is more varied than that of men.
- Women use more diminutives and use more politically acceptable or appropriate words than men.
- Adjectives and qualifiers are used more by women.
- Women speak more indirectly than men.
- Women are more easily interrupted in speech than men.
- Women use more nonverbal communication.
- Male language is clear, direct and precise.

Within the different types of oral communication between a man and a woman, there is a similarity in the characteristics of the left and right hemisphere of the brain, with the left side guided by reason, the objective and facts, and the right dominated by details, art, the emotional. By nature they work together creating a whole, respecting their exclusive characteristics and functions, which is why the solution to communication problems, suggests psychotherapist Pérez Pino, is to know how to recognize the language used by the other and to be able to use both languages to have more amplitude in the relationship. Through the language of facts and the language of what we feel while those facts are happening, in this way it is clear that showing emotions without fear, in a balanced and timely manner is a guarantee for a positive relationship (Bautista, 2011).

As Bautista Pino mentions, understanding the different styles of oral communication between men and women is beneficial for conflict resolution in marriages. Sometimes it is perceived that the member of the female sex is unhappy with her spouse's lack of initiative, triggering emotions of frustration.

Although Bautista mentions the differences in communication between the sexes, a study conducted on 1,400 human brains ruled out that there is an anatomical difference based on sex. The scientists who carried out the research pointed out that there is no region of the brain that shows any distinction between the male and female brain (Criado, 2015). Studies have noted the difference in the nature of communication between the sexes, and from a physiological perspective, no inequalities are found in the brain, so it is perceived that the differences in communication could be the result of a transgenerational type of learning, in which aggressive and submissive communication styles are learned, without finding the balance in assertiveness.

Verbal abuse in couples

The problem of verbal abuse in marriage was the initial impetus for an investigation that is now presented as a book. The aim is to understand the causes of this type of behavior, in which shouting and insults are used to attack the individual toward whom one has supposedly sentimental affection, an illogical contradiction to the precepts that guide the feelings of peace and love.

For Barreto (2011), to mistreat is to diminish a positive quality of a person, to reduce, damage or hurt this person; verbal mistreatment is part of emotional mistreatment, where physical aggression, abuse or neglect cause a psychological problem of emotional wounding. Barreto points out that this type of mistreatment can severely affect the person in a negative way, through the use of the language used in communication and interpersonal dialogue; language that is denigrating, rude, manipulative, humiliating or abusive, depending on the intention of the speaker, can be a matter of life or death, of construction or destruction.

A study of 45 Venezuelan families indicates that within couple conflicts, the type of aggression that occurs in verbal fights is personal insults at 44.06 percent, ranking first in order of frequency, with denigration of the partner ranking second at 25.42 percent (Rodríguez & Córdova, 2009). Contextualizing the statistics, the word "insulting" comes from Latin and refers to the action of offending someone by provoking and irritating them with words or actions (Real Academia Española). For their part, García (2008, as cited in Tabernero, 2010) considers that insulting is an expressive eloquent act, which is characterized by the fact that the sender is indifferent to the interpersonal maintenance of their own image, but very sensitive to the degradation of the image of others.

As the study of 45 Venezuelan families points out, insulting the other is the first negative action that takes place when an argument occurs, attacking aggressively with insensitivity, without using reflection, analysis or control. This suggests a lack of mental, emotional and physiological connection, which is perceived as not having been of interest to be taught or contemplated by educational institutions.

For some people, offending and insulting could be the same thing, although they are actually not. According to Stamateas (2012), an offense can be caused by something that is done or by omission, an expectation that is held and not fulfilled. This can be painful as it represents an action against the other person. The person may not mean to harm; the intention is to draw attention to themselves in order to provoke a bad emotional reaction. The intention of an offense as noted, requires provoking attention in a negative way, which continues to indicate a primitive behavior where ignorance prevails. As Barreto (2011) points out, the offender chooses to use expressions that cause a lot of damage, such as the following:

- You are good for nothing.
- I curse the day I met you.
- You're a fool.
- You'll never get ahead.
- May life repay you with the worst.

- I'll see you sink to the ground.
- If you were like ... you'd do better.
- If you don't do as I say ... I don't love you, I won't go on with you, you won't have my help...
- From you nothing more can be expected ... nothing good.

Barreto points out some of the reasons why people use this type of negative behavior:

1. They believe they have control and authority over everything.
2. In their child, they received no education in language.
3. They have fears and deep wounds that they now want to use as revenge.
4. They believe they have knowledge, truth and reason in all things.
5. They surround themselves with people who use obscene, outrageous language.
6. They have no self-control; they are intolerant and express criticism without thinking first.

When a couple is in a conflict or a short argument and a fight breaks out with shouting or an inflexible silence, each of the individuals is determined to win; both individuals want to show that they feel hurt and that they are right, so the communication channels are damaged or completely disrupted (Gottman & Silver, 2010).

From his perspective, Stamateas (2012) points out that a person is mature when he or she has the ability to not get discouraged or feel affected when offended, insulted, denigrated, shouted at or mistreated. If the concept of maturity mentioned by Stamateas is considered, then people who find themselves in a dynamic of emotional violence are immature and therefore lack emotional intelligence.

The ideal response to such behaviors is to learn an assertive communication style that can stand in the middle of a passive-aggressive conflict resolution style; however, a study of 650 couples found that happily married couples report having shouting matches and say that such discussions have not damaged their marriage. Conflict resolution does not make a marriage work (Gottman &

Silver, 2010). According to Gottman and Silver, the authors of this study, common interests and respect for these interests bring people together. Couples report that they have different conflict styles: some avoid fighting all the time, some argue all the time, some solve issues through dialogue and compromise without raising their voices, so there is no general pattern. Every couple is different. The problem arises when one partner wants to solve an issue through dialogue and the other through avoidance or vice versa. The key to a happy marriage is to find a partner who agrees with the other person. If a person has problems with authority and his wife is authoritarian, the result will be disastrous, so he will have to have as a partner a person who does not try to dominate him (Gottman & Silver, 2010).

Faced with these different types of perspectives, where some authors point out that verbal abuse deeply harms individuals, and other authors indicate that marriages which have this type of behavior show happiness, the idea that emerges is the naturalization of violence and the lack of understanding of the concept of happiness that the individual subjects in the study have. A concept of happiness that is not associated with or related to the principles of the culture of peace is observed, since for no reason does violent dialogue turn out to be an axis of peace, unless we delve deeper into studies where the compatibility of character is a component that favors peace within marriages, as by complementing each other there is no need to resolve conflicts, therefore, there will be no arguments or violence.

Assertive oral communication

The origin of the word "assertiveness", according to Robredo, derives from the Latin *asserere* or *assertum*, which means to state or defend. For their part, Rodríguez and Serralde refer to and define assertiveness as meaning the affirmation of one's own personality, self-confidence, self-esteem, poise, and confident and efficient communication (Gaeta & Galvanovskis, 2009).

It is behavioral theories that provide assertive techniques, based on the principle that when a person modifies his or her actions, he or she also modifies his or her attitudes and feelings. Therefore, it is possible to develop strategies to change behavior, regardless of the unconscious motives that lead to it, whether through self-assertion or assertiveness techniques found in the field of behavioral psychology (Naranjo, 2008). Regarding the definition of assertiveness, it will be defined as a possible behaviorist technique for the development of relationships that promote the components of peace within marriage, following the precept of the psychosociological school that proposes aggressive and violent behavior in the face of conflict as the result of learning, not something natural for the human being (Ruiz, 2006).

For the psychologist Olga Castanyer (n.d., as cited in Pérez de las Heras, 2010), the definition of assertiveness is clearer and she suggests it is the ability to assert one's own rights and opinions without manipulating or allowing someone else's manipulation, indicating high self-esteem as a sign of assertiveness in the person.

Some time ago, authors such as Rodríguez and Serralde (1991, as cited in (Gaeta & Galvanovskis, 2009) stated that assertiveness was the same as self-esteem, or at least was a component of it. Therefore, there are coincidences in the relationship between assertiveness and the degree of consideration that one has for oneself. In reference to the definition of assertiveness, Riso (2002) suggests in a simple way, it is the ability to defend and exercise personal rights, for example the ability to say no, to express disagreement, to give a different opinion, to externalize negative emotions without allowing oneself to be manipulated as the submissive person does, or to violate the rights of others as the aggressive person does.

The possibility represented by assertive techniques that favor the construction of a language which helps establish dialogue based on respect, is useful for the creation of a model of peaceful communication, particularly in couple relationships. The main objective is to support harmonious coexistence within marriage, without ensuring the longevity of the marriage, but to block the use of violence for the duration of the union.

Characteristics of assertive oral communication

According to some psychological studies, within human relationships there are three forms of responses to interpersonal relationships.

The first is the anxious getaway, the second the assertive response and last the aggressive response, which are described below (Aguilar & Vargas, 2010).

The *anxious getaway* is characterized by a person behaving passively, allowing their rights to be violated allowing others to take advantage of them; not achieving their goals, feeling frustrated, unhappy, hurt and anxious; being inhibited and withdrawn; and having other people make decisions for them.

In the *assertive response* a person protects their own rights and respects those of others; they achieve their goals without detriment to others; they feel good about themselves and are confident; they are sociable and emotionally expressive; they make their own decisions.

Aggressive responses include violating the rights of others; achieving goals at the expense of others; being belligerent; humiliating and belittling others; being explosive, unpredictable, hostile and angry; and meddling in the decisions of others.

The assertive response, as can be observed, is somewhere in between the anxious (passive) and the aggressive response. There is no inactivity, but nor are limits exceeded in such a way that violence or aggression exists. In today's marriages, there is a perceived lack of this middle ground of responses in marital cohabitation. The statistics tip the balance in favor of passivity and aggressiveness on the part of those involved. Assertiveness in oral communication is the expression of a profound self-knowledge, in which self-esteem has an active function, since the individual recognizes his or her strengths, knows his or her weaknesses, but works on them to preserve the central point of emotional balance that allows him or her to develop confidence and security.

The need to direct speech through education toward greater assertiveness is one of the manifest proposals of this book, giving language the importance it deserves as a guiding element for the creation of violence-free relationships within marriage. Within the characteristics of the assertive communication model, authors such as Aguilar and Vargas (2010) point to a series of assertive rights that people should be aware of in order to claim them and improve the type of relationships they establish around them, identifying the following:

1. Sometimes you have the right to be first.
2. You can make mistakes.
3. You have the right to be the judge of your feelings and accept them as valid.
4. You can have your own opinions.
5. You have the right to change your direction or your mind.
6. You can protest about something you think is unfair.
7. You have the right to interrupt to ask for clarification.
8. You have the right to try to make a change.
9. You have the right to ask for emotional support.
10. You have the right to express and feel pain.
11. You have the right to ignore others.
12. You have the right to receive recognition for a job well done.
13. You have the right to say no.
14. You have the right to be alone when others want company.
15. You have the right to not anticipate the wants and needs of others.
16. You have the right to not be beholden to the goodwill of others.
17. You have the right to respond or not to respond.

Continuing with the exploration of assertive rights, clinical psychologist Elia Roca Villanueva (2005) mentions that we have the right to:

1. Be our own judges.
2. Choosing whether or not to take responsibility for the problems of others.
3. Decide whether or not to give explanations.
4. Change our mind.
5. Make mistakes.
6. Say "I don't know".
7. Not need approval from others.
8. Make decisions without logic.
9. Not understand other people's expectations.
10. Not try to be a perfect person.

Roca identifies a series of assertive rights that are perceived to reflect characteristics of security, autonomy, decisiveness and non-emotional dependence. What is significant in the set of guidelines they propose has a connection with the human essence, which reflects a human being with a mission of continuous learning and full acceptance of his or her mistakes. They reflect the allowance of painful emotions, the relocation of ideas to change paths without the need for explanation, the value of freedom in action and thought to express or not to express, to coexist or not to coexist, since opting for the assertive communication model is a matter of self-esteem and self-knowledge. Other characteristics related to assertiveness mentions are the right to say no, the continuous acceptance of people's proposals even if they go against what one really thinks or wants to do, can incite the development of abuse and manipulation, turning the person into a human puppet, losing one of the most important values of the human being: dignity (Riso, 2002).

For Vilchis Contreras (2015, as cited in Vargas, 2015), psychologist and consultant, people who find themselves in the circle of non-assertiveness have self-esteem problems, as they are people who seek acceptance and recognition from those around them. Not being able to say "no" is synonymous with low self-confidence. How can not being able to say "no" have an impact on the culture of peace within a marriage? In trying to answer this question, the importance lies in the content of the word. The expression "no" brings with it the capacity for high self-esteem, appreciation and respect for thoughts, needs or requirements. This very self-consideration, depending on whether it is positive or negative, makes the exchange of peaceful or violent messages within the marriage permeable. According to sexologist and therapist Gladys Elena Bonifaz (2013, as cited in Grajales, 2013), in a macho society like Mexico's, some men express their insecurities and fears through violence, which is connected to the aggressor's self-esteem and the victim's submission.

On the subject of assertiveness, as the aforementioned authors have pointed out, it can be concluded that assertive language is the result of good self-esteem, which is why, as a first step, self-knowledge is required, or the ability to answer several questions: Who are you? What are your likes and dislikes? What emotions prevail in your day? The assertive person needs to have clear priorities, attitudes of respect toward oneself and courtesy toward others. After having identified the need to increase self-esteem, through a continuous process of individual review that includes self-knowledge as a first step to generate an assertive language, it is necessary to explore how to talk assertively, what to say, what not to say and how to say it to other people.

What to say, what not to say and how to say it

This section deals with suggestions and techniques for expressing messages following an assertive communication model. Several authors suggest the most appropriate way to ask for a request, how to speak in situations of annoyance, and how to send the right message to achieve the desired objective instead of mentioning wrong phrases that aggravate a situation, achieving negative results or repetitive behaviors.

In order to improve interaction with other people, Aguilar and Vargas (2010) suggest that the following skills have to be learned: identifying one's communication style—submissive, assertive or aggressive—identifying assertive rights, developing a rational philosophy of life and learning some competences. They mention the following:

- Stand up for your rights.
- Ask for changes in other people's behavior.
- Ask for favors.
- Say no.
- Give compliments.
- Make a complaint.
- Make decisions.
- Act in conflict.
- Argue and negotiate.
- Walk away from inappropriate relationships or people.

Aguilar and Vargas (2010) agree that the first step to being assertive is to know one's rights; self-knowledge is also important, since one has to find a point of honesty with oneself in order to define what type of communication is commonly carried out: is it aggressive; is it passive? This is when the question arises: how, then, does one make these changes after identifying that the communication model which one has had all one's life is not the most adequate and is far from being assertive? To try to answer this question, studies have examined various message strategies that promote greater understanding with others. Among the basic principles to achieve assertive communication in a couple, Castanyer (2011, as cited in Aguilar & Vargas, 2010) suggests the following:

1. Make a request instead of making a demand.
2. Ask questions instead of making accusations
3. When criticizing someone else, talk about what they do, not who they are.
4. Stop accumulating negative emotions; don't let them remain uncommunicated.
5. Discuss issues one by one; don't take advantage and express reproach about more things that bother you.
6. Do not generalize, using words like always or never.
7. Always think before you say something, making sure that the consequences are positive.
8. Verbal communication should be congruent with nonverbal communication.

Castanyer notes that in order to manifest this type of principles, it is necessary to develop certain communication skills with one's partner. She mentions the following:

- Giving compliments: to say "thank you" and also to show appreciation by giving material gifts.
- Thanking for compliments: this refers to showing joy at a gift or a verbal compliment.
- Asking for compliments: this is when you tell the other person what is required.
- Expressing negative feelings: this means, when there are emotions of sadness or anger, always communicate them in an assertive way, not showing a victim mask, and speak at the right time using "I" messages, saying, "I feel sad when you don't pick up your clothes" instead of "You never pick up your clothes".

- Empathizing: is putting yourself in your partner's shoes and observing their problems.
- Exchanging physical affection: this does not only refer to sexual exchange; it is about hugging, kissing, being close to the partner.
- Dealing with unexpected hostility or bad moods: not everything in a couple's life is sweetness; there are also moments of anger due to issues unrelated to the couple. Therefore, an assertive person can react in two ways:
  - Repeated assertiveness, refers to using the broken record technique: in which the non-irritated person responds with an "I" message, saying "I have nothing to do with your bad mood" or "I am not going to lose a good night because you are in a bad mood".
  - Empathic assertiveness: this starts with putting oneself in the other person's shoes, using phrases such as "you seem to be very upset tonight", and then emphasizing a constructive assertive phrase firmly, "but I think that anger is coming from other people and I am not responsible for that".

The psychologist Haim Ginott (n.d., as cited in Pérez, 2010) uses a technique very similar to the one mentioned by Canstanyer to communicate assertively. He created the XYZ technique in order to establish a type of communication that is productive. This type of strategy consists of resolving a conflict by saying: "when you make X, you make me feel Y, although I would have liked to feel Z". An example of this type of message elaboration would be: "when you go away with your friends and don't inform me, you make me feel that you don't care about me and I worry; I would like to feel confident and that you are interested in my peace of mind".

López (2015) provides other rules that are developed within international agreements and meetings, in which through each intervention, the following must be done in order to obtain productive results:

- Be brief, concise and clear.
- Use the opinions of others, being discreet and confidential.
- Respect others; do not follow personal attacks.

- Call things by their name.
- Always talk about the problem and not about the person.
- See yourself as a learner.
- Value silences.
- Avoid cross-talk.
- Give credit for what is said.
- Disregard stereotypes.

Among the coincidences suggested by Aguilar and Vargas (2010) and López (2015), the aforementioned authors is the importance of establishing messages in a concrete and clear way about the action and not about the subject, always establishing a brain–mouth connection, which requires skills such as the management of emotions in order to exercise self-control. It could be simple to practice the above when there are no latent conflicts within the couple's relationship, but human relationships are complex. Daily coexistence brings with it different points of view and perceptions of realities in which the struggle to defend each one's point of view is an ideal way to violence in any of its typologies.

Authors such as Lozano (2015) mention that arguing is an art; it requires acquiring various skills such as differentiating with whom you are arguing, doing it in private, obtaining a dose of humility, making the other person feel important, using time-out and always remaining calm. For Cala (2015), it is not only necessary to control one's emotions, but it is also necessary to cultivate the virtue of sincerity, since in order to be sincere with others, it is necessary to start with oneself. If a person does not accept him- or herself as he or she is, self-deception is an obstacle in relating to others. Cala also stresses that it is always necessary to be honest. What he suggests is that one should ask oneself: is it the right time, place and moment? These questions should be answered, and if the answer is positive, there is no need to mistreat someone. When you are sincere, you can be gentle and warm but firm. He also makes a number of suggestions for dialogue:

- Be open-minded and open to dialogue, to listen to all kinds of arguments, even if you do not agree with them.

- Critical sincerity should always go hand in hand with highlighting the positive aspects, not just focusing on the negative ones.
- Never leave a negative opinion in the air without offering positive solutions.
- The responsibility that comes with being honest is an element that must be handled with prudence and intelligence.

According to what Lozano and Cala suggest, it can be concluded that there are different perspectives in terms of being able to establish assertive communication; their contributions suggest that positive thinking about the will to solve a conflict is fundamental. In addition to investing in self-knowledge, which will allow one to know what one wants, to prioritize and to be able to express the right words with an intonation conducive to mutual understanding, it is also essential to reprogram the linguistic system to which one is accustomed.

Neurolinguistic programming

In order to reprogram the use of language, the study of neurolinguistic programming is indispensable. An understanding of the concept is required, which some authors have described as a communication strategy, a style or a discipline. But the real question is: What is neurolinguistic programming? And what does it consist of?

The concept of neurolinguistic programming—NLP—was proposed in the 1970s by John Grinder and Richard Blander. Its definition goes beyond a set of tools that originate from linguistics, Gestalt therapy, general semantics, transactional analysis and the body, cognitive and emotional domains (Jaruffe & Pomares, 2011). Forner (2014) defines it as a practical discipline that helps human beings to use their resources correctly, to relearn who they are, to use their abilities to the maximum to improve their performance, to manipulate negative situations in a positive way in order to take advantage of failures and to advance continuously. For Pacheco (2004), NLP is based on certain principles:

- Any biologically feasible behavior can be programmed.
- The way to internalize experiences is through language.
- The means to obtain change is by generating new alternatives.
- Any behavior has a positive intention.
- The human composition is made up of its own resources and goals.

The importance of self-knowledge as a basis to replace negative linguistic expressions is recognized. In order to be able to replace negative linguistic expressions, it is necessary to determine and detail the area of opportunity in order to replace them with words that work and are in accordance with the main objective, which is to achieve an assertive communication style that results in a dialogue based on nonviolence within the marriage.

Similar to NLP within peace studies, Johan Galtung (n.d., as cited in Calderón, 2009) proposes the theory of transcendence and transformation, for which he points out three elements that are found in every conflict: attitudes, behavior and contradiction. After analyzing them to be able to carry out a transformation, it is required to apply empathy, nonviolence and creativity. It is observed within NLP the transformation and creativity that Galtung addresses as one of the ways to find peace, for NLP every expression has a positive intention, the same is related to the studies of the structural school, where the nonviolent nature of the human being is the focus.

The individual usually communicates using poor expression, which is called superficial structure, in which there are omissions, generalizations and distortions (Jaruffe & Pomares, 2011). The concept presented by these authors points to the clear example of the deficit theory, which addresses the problem of ignorance in communication tools that results in violence. The human being learns it because he or she simply does not know peace. Forner (2014) reiterates the support of NLP, which lies in the fact that all words have a positive intention, as previously mentioned. What makes it difficult for the correct purpose to come to light is that it is hidden in negative phrases that are continually used in the usual way, so

Table 2.1 Neurolinguistic programming exercises

Negative NLP word or idea	Magical NLP word or idea
Being fat	Abundance in movement
Fired	Open to new experiences.
Stressed	¡Hawai is calling me!
Being poor in money	Rich Future
Failure	Surprise result.
Cancer	Opportunity to heal my life.
To have a cold	To be cleaning up.
Divorce	Opportunity to be happy.

Source: Forner (2014).

he proposes a series of exercises to reprogram the correct way of expressing situations, moods and so forth (see Table 2.1).

Bandler and Grinder offer a series of verbal strategies that are aligned with the principles of NLP (Jaruffe & Pomares, 2011):

Generalization: when the person does not express a specific action. An example is: people keep bothering me. This is a generalization in which you have to work with specifying verbs that the subject is not expressing.

Omission: is the process of selecting some dimensions but eliminating others. The subject is required to finish the missing sentence. For example when someone expresses: I am scared, he or she does not finish the sentence, so the person is encouraged to specify and enrich with details the particular situation.

Distortion: is the action of placing responsibility on others whether it be a person, emotion, animal or thing for issues that are within one's control. For example, the individual might express: the student makes me angry, meaning a sentence with distortion, as the anger they are experiencing is attributed to someone else, when it is not that person who is experiencing that negative emotion.

According to Villoria (n.d., as cited in Jaruffe & Pomares, 2011), these mechanisms of language structure and communication act directly on the individual's belief system. As emphasized in transactional analysis, when the subject uses it as a norm in his life, it is because the individual is required to detail his generalizations, complete the missing omissions in his reality and correct the distortions he or she makes.

NLP of the individual is an issue in conjunction with assertive communication, which are aligned with peace studies. It is essential to apply tools to people to help complement the language deficit that is perceived in Mexico, based on the statistics of emotional violence in couples. It is complex to tackle the problem of language as it involves a series of factors that are deeply linked to the self, such as: self-esteem, self-knowledge, self-awareness, willingness to change. Moreover, it is a matter of education, which is the responsibility of both parents and the curricula of educational institutions. However, educability is a quality of being human, so a person can learn all the time and this makes change possible.

Reflection questions skill I

1. What is speech and with which person did it appear?
2. What is linguistics?
3. What is the purpose of language? What is paralinguistics?
4. What is assertiveness?
5. Mention the three forms of responses for dealing with interpersonal relationships.
6. Write the basic principles for assertive communication in couples
7. What is neurolinguistic programming?
8. Indicate the principles of neurolinguistic programming.
9. Indicate some neurolinguistic programming exercises.

References

Aguila Carralero, A. (2010). *Consideraciones acerca de la importancia del empleo del lenguaje no verbal para el exitoso desempeño profesional jurista.* Recuperado el 9 de diciembre de 2015, de Revista del Instituto de Ciencias Jurídicas: www.redalyc.org/pdf/2932/293222977011.pdf

Aguilar Morales, J. E., & Vargas, J. E. (2010). *Comunicación Asertiva.* Recuperado el 17 de noviembre de 2014, de Asociación Oaxaquena de Psicología A.C: www.conductitlan.net/psicologia_organizacional/comunicacion_asertiva.pdf

Bally, C. (1977). *El lenguaje y la vida.* Buenos Aires: Losada S.A.

Barreto, A. (2011). *Tóxicos Emocionales.* Madrid: CCS.

Bautista Pino, J. (17 de octubre de 2011). *Hombres y mujeres, dos formas de comunicarse.* Recuperado el 16 de noviembre de 2014, de El Rincón de la Ciencia y la Tecnología: Un blog dedicado a la difusión científica y tecnológica: http://elrincondelacienciaytecnologia.blogspot.mx/2011/10/por-que-hombres-y-mujeres-hablan-de.html

Burke, P. (2001). *Hablar y Callar.* Barcelona: Gedisa, S.A.

Cala, I. (2015). *Hablar con Franqueza.* Recuperado el 24 de noviembre de 2015, de Cala Enterprises: http://ismaelcala.com/hablar-con-franqueza/

Calderón Concha, P. (2009). *Teoría de conflictos de Johan Galtung.* Recuperado el 27 de abril de 2016, de Revista de paz y conflictos: www.ugr.es/~revpaz/tesinas/rpc_n2_2009_dea3.pdf

Criado, M. Á. (1 de diciembre de 2015). *No hay un cerebro masculino y otro femenino.* Recuperado el 8 de diciembre de 2015, de El Pais: http://elpais.com/elpais/2015/11/30/ciencia/1448904392_009014.html?id_externo_rsoc=FB_CM

Defleur, M., Kearney, P., Plax, T., & DeFleur, M. (2005). *Fundamentos de comunicación humana.* Cuidad de México: McGraw Hill.

Escamilla Morales, J., & Vega, G. (2012). *Miradas multidisciplinarias a los fenómenos de cortesía y descortesía en el mundo hispánico.* Barranquilla: Universidad de Atlántico-Programa EDICE.

Fajardo Uribe, L. (julio-diciembre de 2009). *A propósito de la comunicación no verbal.* Obtenido de Forma y Función: www.redalyc.org/articulo.oa?id=21916691006

Forner, R. (2014). *PNL para todos.* Cuidad de México: Lectorum.

Gaeta González, L., & Galvanovskis Kasparane, A. (julio–diciembre de 2009). *Asertividad: Un análisis teórico-empírico.* Recuperado el 17 de noviembre de 2014, de Enseñanza e Investigación en Psicología: www.redalyc.org/pdf/292/29211992013.pdf

García García, N. (diciembre de 2008). *El Proceso de la Comunicación y el Lenguaje.* Recuperado el 3 de diciembre de 2015, de Inovación y Experiencias educativas: www.csi-csif.es/andalucia/modules/mod_ense/revista/pdf/Numero_13/NOELIAM_GARCIA_2.pdf

Gottman, J. M., & Silver, N. (2010). *Siete reglas de oro para vivir en pareja: Un estudio exhaustivo sobre las relaciones y la convivencia.* Barcelona: Debolsillo. 0#v=onepage&q=gritos%20en%20la%20pareja&f=false

Grajales, I. (28 de septiembre de 2013). *Un México de machos y mujeres sumisas: GB.* Recuperado el 2015, de Noticiasnet: www.noticiasnet.mx/portal/general/salud/172672-un-m%C3%A9xico-de-machos-y-mujeres-sumisas-gb

Jaruffe Romero, A., & Pomares Jacquin, M. (agosto de 2011). *Programación Neurolinguistica. Realidad o Mito de la Psicología y las Ciencias Cognitivas.* Recuperado el 1 de diciembre de 2015, de Universidad de Magdalena Revista de la Facultad de Ciencias de la Salud: dialnet.unirioja.es/descarga/articulo/3903314.pdf

Locke, J. (2011). *Duels and Duets. Why Men and Women Talk So Differently.* Cambridge: Cambridge University Press:

López Follegatti, J. (2015). *Diálogos que transforman.* Cuidad de México: CARE Perú.

Lozano, C. (2015). *No te enganches.* Lima, Peru: Aguilar.

Maldonado Willman, H. (1998). *Manual de comunicación oral*. Cuidad de México: Longman de México Editores, S.A. de C.V.
Naranjo Pereira, M. (enero-abril de 2008). *Relaciones interpersonales adecuadas mediante una comunicación y conducta asertivas*. Recuperado el 17 de noviembre de 2014, de Revista Electrónica Actualidades Investigativas en Educación: www.redalyc.org/articulo.oa?id=44780111
Pacheco Pulido, G. (2004). *Mediación, Cultura de la Paz*. Puebla: Porrúa.
Pérez de las Heras, M. (2010). *¿Estás Comunicando?* Madrid: LID.
Real Academia Española. (2001). *Real Academia Española*. Recuperado el 29 de octubre de 2014, de Diccionario de la Real Academia Española: http://lema.rae.es/drae/?val=lenguaje
Real Academia Española. (s.f.). *Real Academia Española*. Recuperado el 27 de julio de 2015, de Insultar: http://buscon.rae.es/drae/srv/search?id=TYBrn9nPeDXX24uhlN0O
Riso, W. (2002). *Cuestión de Dignidad. Aprenda a decir NO y gane autoestima siendo asertivo*. Bogotá and Barcelona: Editorial Norma.
Roca Villanueva, E. (2005). *Cómo mejorar tus habilidades sociales*. Obtenido de Colegio Oficial de Psicólogos: http://eoepsabi.educa.aragon.es/descargas/F_Educacion_emocional/f_7_autoestima/f_7.3.Programas/1.3.Programa%20autoestima%20hhss.pdf
Rodríguez, F., & Córdova, L. (mayo-junio de 2009). *Violencia en la pareja: manifestaciones concretas y factores asociados*. Recuperado el 1 de diciembre de 2015, de Espacio Abierto: www.redalyc.org/pdf/122/12211826007.pdf
Rosenberg, M. B. (2006). *Comunicaciòn no violenta, un lenguaje de vida*. Cuidad de Mèxico: Fusiòn.
Ruiz, Y. (2006). *análisis y resolución de conflictos desde una dimensión psicosocial*. Obtenido de Universitat Jaume I: www.uji.es/bin/publ/edicions/jfi12/19.pdf
Silva Salguero, J. C. (enero de 2006). *Cuadernos de Lingüística Hispánica*. Recuperado el 29 de octubre de 2014, de El lenguaje duele -Algunas relaciones entre conocimiento y lenguaje: www.redalyc.org/articuloBasic.oa?id=322230192010
Stamateas, B. (2012). *No me maltrates*. Barcelona: B de Bolsillo .
Tabernero Sala, C. (2010). *Injurias, maldiciones y juramentos en la lengua española del siglo XVII*. Recuperado el 27 de julio de 2015, de Revista de Lexicografía: http://ruc.udc.es/dspace/bitstream/2183/8441/1/RL%2016%202010%20art%207.pdf
Vargas, I. (15 de junio de 2015). *Claves para saber decir 'no' en el trabajo*. Obtenido de CNN en expansión: www.cnnexpansion.com/mi-carrera/2015/06/12/claves-para-aprender-a-decir-no-en-el-trabajo
Verderber, R. F., & Verderber, K. S. (2005). *Comunícacte*. Cuidad de México: Thomson.
Xbalanqué, V. (15 de mayo de 2012). *Violencia emocional, física, sexual y económica*. Recuperado el 16 de noviembre de 2014, de Secretaria de Gobernación: www.violenciaenlafamilia.conapo.gob.mx/en/Violencia_Familiar/Violencia_emocional_fsica_sexual_y_econmica

Chapter 3

Skill 2
Active listening

The art of listening

Addressing the subject of listening represents, as the title indicates, an art, because it is an activity carried out by the human being, in which the aim is to express or communicate. In the same way, listening is a nonverbal communication process where the body sends constant messages, conveying as a result the creation of an atmosphere of interest or disinterest in the cycle of communication and daily coexistence. Studies reveal that human beings spend more time listening than speaking; of the total time spent on communication, 22 percent is spent on reading and writing, 23 percent on speaking and 55 percent on listening. This does not mean that there is more willingness to listen than to speak, but rather that there is greater exposure to receiving information than to transmitting it (Codina Jiménez, 2004).

Human dynamics are complex to understand; people talk about different topics, give their opinions, express their thoughts. There is an unstoppable desire to talk about their needs, ambitions, dreams, frustrations and requirements, but a reduced willingness to listen to others and to themselves. When it comes to the skill of listening, it is not only about the interpersonal relationship, but about a larger dimension, the ability to see the mind–body connection in order to listen, to analyze the deepest feelings and emotions. At present, there is a perceived imbalance in communication, which can lead to violence in couples. One of these problems is the lack of listening, a skill without which it is difficult to reach an understanding and, consequently, the action of resolving conflicts and reaching

DOI: 10.4324/9781003207023-4

agreements in a peaceful way can be a challenge for the coexistence of the couple.

Interestingly, skills or deficiencies communicate the constitution of an individual. The way a person can listen reveals different aspects of his or her personality, character and background. Taking González A. (2011) as a reference, four profiles of temperament and level of listening that humans can adopt are described:

The first is the blood motivator profile, which corresponds to the lowest level of listening. These individuals are very extroverted, motivational and excellent at speaking quickly and communicating in public. They always manage to be the center of attention, their thinking capacity is very fast, and they do not allow the other person to speak because they are never silent.

The second personality corresponds to the pragmatic type, which is choleric with a low level of listening. These are practical people, indifferent listeners. They are interested in fulfilling an objective, they project themselves as blunt and calculating because they like to give orders, to command without listening to the feelings and emotions of the people around them.

The third is the perfectionist with a melancholic personality, which corresponds to a medium level of listening. They are analytical, introverted and their main obstacle to listening is to adopt a negative stance; their critical nature compels them to needs for excellence and perfection, which drives them to always respond negatively.

The last profile is the peaceful one, with a phlegmatic temperament and a high listening level; this person has the ability to remain calm in the face of adversity, does not interrupt or argue, prefers discretion, enjoys listening to others and has conciliatory skills, and is distressed when it is his turn to speak.

In order to improve one's listening skills, the first step is to identify one's profile and temperament. This type of dynamic would be beneficial if the areas of opportunity were identified and strengthened from childhood so that in adult life, communication would be of higher quality. Satir (2015) notes that, if communication is developed in a congruent and meaningful way, it will attract positive consequences. Communication patterns can be learned and taught, because all people have internal resources that can be used inventively so that communication favors satisfactory relationships. It is through the five rights shown below, that a person develops with an integral structure. These five rights favor living in a more complete and creative way:

1. The right to see and hear all that exists in the moment, not what should have been, will be or was in the past.
2. The right to express what the person feels and thinks.
3. The right to feel what one wants to feel, rather than what one should feel.
4. The right to ask for what the person wants.
5. The right to take risks.

Educability is one of the characteristics of the human being, so it is possible to learn to listen not only to another person but also to begin to listen carefully to thoughts and emotions; and to understand the body's communication, conditioning and mental patterns in order to generate self-knowledge that benefits coexistence with oneself and, consequently, with others. When mentioning the term "listening", whose relevance has been pointed out above, it is convenient to define it as it is usually used, as a synonym of the verb to hear, without identifying that each of these terms has a different nature. Although both use the sense of hearing, they each have a particular nature.

Hear or listen

Bair and Knower (n.d., as cited in McEntee & Férnandez, 1993) refer to this difference and point out that listening is not the same as hearing. The concept of hearing is described as a matter of sensory capacity, while listening is an active process involving perception, comprehension and other mental functions. Among the purposes of listening are to empathize, to be informed and to evaluate. According to Bair and Knower, the basic rules for effective listening are: to know oneself, to be polite, to develop interest in various areas of knowledge, to be physically prepared, to be objective, to be analytical and to try to evaluate. It is a complex list of requirements, especially when emotions such as anger are involved in everyday life, so continuous training is desirable.

Maldonado (1998) defined hearing as simply capturing the sounds that occur in our environment, while listening is hearing with special attention, that is, carefully capturing the sounds that are perceived. When a person is listening he or she employs two key elements: understanding and state of mind. Maldonado considers that a person is listening when he or she demonstrates with his or her actions or reactions that there is complete understanding or precise comprehension of what the message received expresses. On the other hand, state of mind is an element that allows one to hear exactly what was sent; if one's mind is no OK, the message is ignored or twisted, since it determines the degree of openness and attention to the message.

It is the emotional state that interferes with the listening process, since when someone is happy, he or she listens differently than when he or she is angry, sad, worried, calm or melancholic, among other states of mind. Listening is having the mood to understand the message received (Maldonado, 1998). Emotions not only interfere with the listening process, but they also represent a social problem, since emotional violence, positioned according to statistics as the main cause of violence in Mexican society, indicates that there is still much to learn and heal in the area of emotions. Developing emotional intelligence is a subject that should be included in the basic education of all children.

Continuing with those negative aspects that hinder the process of receiving the sender's message, generating noise, lack of attention and understanding, González (2015) describes some vices, defects and negative habits that result in blocking and inhibiting listening among people: the first of the impediments to listening is egocentrism, a very common vice in the communication process of people; individualism, is when a person is interested in talking about themselves and not in giving time to others to be heard. Nowadays, another factor is social networks that centralize one's attention, preventing listening. This second factor is isolation, which occurs when a person distances themselves from others and focuses their

108 Skill 2: Active listening

attention on their own interests, as reflected in virtual addiction. Being impulsive and obsessive disables listening on the pretext of not having time, behaviors that inhibit listening.

Other factors are stress and anxiety, the lack of control of which produces a mental tangle in which the subject continually has thoughts related to tasks, commitments, reports and functions to fulfill; his or her nervous system may be on the verge of collapse, so that if someone wants to establish a conversation, he or she could react aggressively. Finally, González observes that a person who behaves noisily and exaggeratedly in order to become the center of attention will not listen. By laughing and shouting boisterously, he or she will not help someone else show off. Finally, someone who engages in distracted and absent-minded behavior, characterized by deep silences, is not used to listening to someone but to look into their own inner complications (see Figure 3.1).

Nowadays, with the use of social networks, there has been an increase in the number of factors that block listening. Its lack of regulation has increased the separation in coexistence. Studies call this "physical presence but absent attention". It is a new form of coexistence in which technology has distanced people from each other. Recent research has attributed the term "phubbing" to the subject, a word that is composed of phone and snubbing. The expression is used to describe a situation in which people choose to use

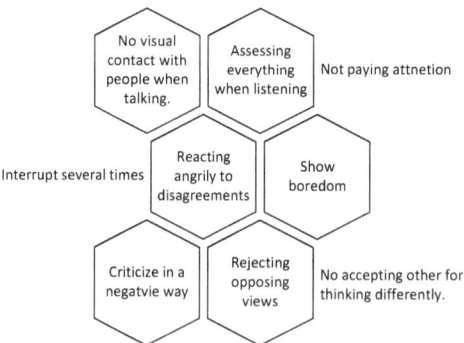

Figure 3.1 Negative listening habits.

Source: Own elaboration based on Gonzalez (2015).

technological devices and reduce their attention to their companions or the people they are living with (Serrano-Puche, 2015).

For Satir (2015), there is a relevant relationship between the way people communicate and their level of self-esteem. The productivity of communication depends on the style used, which can help solve problems in daily life and with the environment or, on the contrary, help hinder solutions to them. In addressing this issue, authors such as Polaino-Lorente (2008) point out that listening is an antidote to violence. The reason for this comes from the peace of mind that comes from being listened to by someone. Polaino-Lorente suggests that when you listen, you have trust in the other person, and that in order to trust another person, it is indispensable to believe that the human species is more positive than negative. The concept of trust that is pointed out adds one more element to the component of listening. Perhaps trust will become a topic for further research.

It can be deduced that the problem of emotional violence in marriage lies in a person's lack of self-esteem. As Redorta (2006) notes in his typology of conflict, the roots come from the self; therefore, by not trusting oneself, one cannot trust one's spouse, a factor that inhibits listening, thereby generating a permeable path to violence (see Figure 3.2).

To return to the concept, trust at home fosters security, or unconditional protection. It is the place where a person is accepted and loved for what he or she is. Nowadays, society requires hope, determination and certainty. For these to exist, it is essential to have the responsibility to be and the commitment to comply with the to do. The infant's learning process is related to trust: the child learns behaviors because he trusts the people who teach him. In this process, the innocence of the new being intervenes, which allows him to be free and strengthen

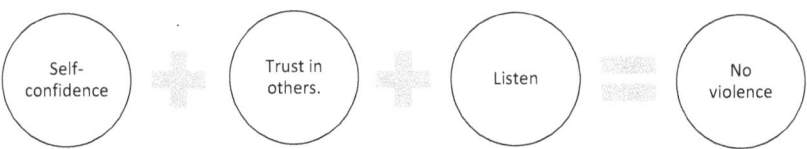

Figure 3.2 Effects of trust and listening.
Source: Own elaboration based on Polaino-Lorente (2008).

human relationships, generating loyalty and sustaining a new social fabric (Polaino-Lorente, 2008). Earlier, in the chapter on assertive language, the relationship between self-esteem and the choice of an assertive communication style was pointed out. Such high self-esteem generates security and confidence, which allows listening to others, thereby favoring peaceful coexistence between people.

Returning to the nature of listening, it is necessary to mention its typology. For authors such as Ortiz (2007), there are different types of listening, such as: appreciative, selective, discerning, analytical, synthesized, empathetic and active. Taking this author as a reference, each type is described with the purpose of understanding its qualities: the first is called appreciative listening, where no attention is paid to listening; it seeks pleasure. Selective listening selects the information that is of interest, while in discerning listening, the main ideas of the message are obtained. Analytical listening makes a study of the relationship of ideas, and in synthesized listening, the receiver takes the initiative in communication. Empathic listening creates the imaginary action of occupying the place of the other. Finally, active listening is that which pays attention to understanding a message in its entirety. It is the most complete of the types because it incorporates the elements of empathic, analytical, synthesized and discerning listening.

The reason for proposing active listening as a component favoring the culture of peace within marriage is due to its broad composition and the benefits obtained from it, which are summarized in a complete understanding of the message and the sender, generating values such as empathy, favoring peace in relationships.

Active listening

The definition of active listening is simple: it is about listening well. It refers to listening with understanding and care. The purpose of this type of listening is to empathize with and understand the sender. It is one of the most basic components of human communication and one of the least manifested in people (Hérnando et al., 2011). Something relevant mentioned by these authors is the lack of active listening in human beings, an essential component of communication that should be present in any information exchange process. On the contrary, it is frequently absent as part of the basic rules of human development that have not been taught in the traditional education system, which focuses attention on school subjects that will rarely be used in everyday or professional life.

Hérnando, Aguaded, and Pérez (2011) indicate that active listening requires adopting an emphatic attitude and performing nonverbal communication behaviors, such as modifying the tone of voice to be softer, maintaining eye contact, making pleasant gestures and having a posture that indicates interest in what the transmitter transmits so that there can be an active type of listening. Active listening favors a series of dynamic postures that the body adopts to send signals of attention, participation, disposition and connection with the transmitter, actions that generate trust in the communication process, creating a harmonious atmosphere, which favors the resolution of conflicts that in other circumstances would be impossible to address.

If active listening were a process, it would have to start with preparing a physical and mental attitude for listening, improving the body position, leaning forward and respecting space. The next aspect is to reinforce the interlocutor with movements or paraphrasing, followed by observation of the other and, finally, the elicitation of main ideas and transmission of feedback.

Taking up another definition of active listening, for Santibáñez (2015), it consists of trying to understand what the other person is saying and making that understanding visible. It requires a sympathetic and pleasant attitude. Active listening requires: respecting silences, reiterating, confronting, clarifying, making obstacles evident and encouraging involvement. Ortiz (2007) finds that active listening necessitates entering the other person's mind and interpreting the message from their point of view. It involves focusing all one's attention on understanding and obtaining the message, as well as the thoughts and emotions of the sender. González (2011) defines it as a type of mature listening that defines people who have developed the virtue of consideration for others. They allow themselves to be nonjudgmental in order to favor the understanding and comprehension of other people's problems, which they consider of equal importance to their own.

Studies indicate that people who can be described in this way have values of solidarity, loyalty, respect, kindness, generosity and self-confidence.

It can be concluded that active listening is the most complete communication style that human beings are capable of adopting. Although it is a type of listening rarely selected by recipients, it appears possible to find it in people with a high level of self-esteem, in those who are able to detach themselves from the need for attention and give their full physical, mental and emotional attention to the sender for a given moment.

Due to the lack of people who opt for this style of active listening, it is advisable to strengthen the component by disseminating the benefits it brings to the communication process and relationships. Continued use of this type of style could probably resolve many interpersonal conflicts, which essentially stem from a lack of attention.

Benefits of active listening

This section aims to point out the benefits that active listening provides to coexistence, specifically in interpersonal relationships, such as those of an affective nature; therefore, the perspective of some authors is reviewed in order to reflect on what they propose and integrate it with the object of study, which is marriage. Among the main utilities that active listening provides, Ortiz (2007) describes the following:

- Creating a positive environment for effective communication.
- Reducing misunderstandings.
- Capturing important information from the sender.
- Learning from the experience of others.
- Evidencing authentic interest in the other person.
- Reducing personal and work-related conflicts.
- Gaining greater trust from the sender.
- Strengthening personal and work relationships.
- Projecting respect for people.

Codina (2004) identifies other bonuses that result from listening:

- Increased self-esteem of the sender, as he or she feels worthy of being heard by someone.
- More effective communication; there is an understanding of thoughts and feelings.
- Reduced possibility of conflict, less risk of misunderstanding.
- One learns from the other person directly.
- A good listener projects an image of respect and intelligence.

Communicators such as Cala (2013) point out that the ability to listen with attention, feeling and critical discernment is the basis of all affective, family and interpersonal relationships. Being listened to is an emotional need. If the relevance of being listened to were fully understood, people would be concerned about being excellent communicators due to the close relationship between active listening and the feeling of love. The consequences that listening generates on an emotional level are positive, productive and create trusting connections that allow reciprocity in interpersonal relationships, specifically within marriage (González, 2015).

Listening is considered a form of communicative care with a healing effect that favors a culture of peace. Communication is part of human nature; it is immersed in movements, gestures and sounds, expressing a message, whether conscious or not. For Muñoz, Ramos and Romera (2012), active listening is no exception, because it implies showing openness toward the person who is expressing something, for that it is necessary to adopt a series of attitudes and behaviors at the level of verbal and nonverbal communication (see Table 3.1).

Table 3.1 Verbal and nonverbal active listening behavior

Attitude	Verbal language	Nonverbal language
Blank mind.	Using monosyllables such as "ajam", "ok", etc	Eye contact.
Attention on each other.	Summarizing the conversation.	Expression of attention.
Effort to understand.	Asking for confirmation of what is understood.	Posture of interest and following.

Source: Own elaboration based on Muñoz et al., 2012.

According to Muñoz, Ramos and Romera, the benefits of active listening lie in the sender and receiver. On the one hand, the sender of the message feels listened to, which creates an atmosphere of trust and improves understanding, and second, the receiver feels useful to others. Among the benefits that active listening generates, the creation of a harmonious atmosphere that originates the acceptance of turns of speech established by common sense is relevant. This process is motivated by the interest that one has in the other person. Without a real interest, you cannot establish active listening.

Silence

Silence is approached in two aspects: the first as the ability to remain silent when someone else is speaking, establishing the element of receiver; the second as the action of remaining silent with oneself, as a technique of self-knowledge, reflection and meditation.

Silence, considered as a discipline of the self, an art with a value similar to that of speech, can become an ally in adopting behaviors of peacefulness, gentleness and moderation, forming part of emotional intelligence. Keeping silence implies quieting down mentally and physiologically in order to find solutions (González, 2011). Silence and active listening are part of a dependent and close relationship; the work that is done in both is what gives rise to the balance in the communication process. Therefore, if the aim is to educate about communication processes, it is essential to start by silencing the tongue and to start listening to the thoughts generated by the mind through silence.

For Hernando, Aguaded, and Pérez (2011), silence can be an indicator of the one who is seeking, encouraging the participation of someone to speak, while at other times it can transmit the sensation of an atmosphere of tension. Silence is therefore a multiple indicator; it depends on the context in which it is developed. It is not only the means by which active listening is manifested, but it is also a messenger of rigidity. Not speaking in some circumstances represents that one does not agree with certain points of view or has insecurity before the issuers, the environment or some factor generating discomfort. In this sense the possibilities are diverse. It could be the uncertainty of the person who is in an environment outside their comfort zone or perhaps it is an introverted and shy personality type.

Scientific studies on the subject of the mind point out that the human being has an average of 60,000 daily thoughts. These can be repetitive or modified. What results from these thoughts is a continuous chain to make judgments about anything without being able to stop (Garcia, 2015). According to this author, the possibility of breaking these chains that generate a constant judgment is feasible by obtaining a focus on the present; with discipline and constancy, positive results can be experienced, directing the attention in a conscious way and not allowing the mind to maintain control.

A subject that generations and ancient cultures have practiced regularly, providing the basis for the balance of their lives, is the control of the mind. When it comes to the mind, it is considered that there is a general lack of knowledge about it, mainly, where is the mind? Who is the mind? Is the mind the creator of thoughts, or is it the brain? Who directs behavior, the self or the mind?

Three centuries ago, René Descartes defined the mind as an extracorporeal entity, which manifests itself in the pineal gland, while psychological research by Neal Miller contributed to biofeedback, which, through a mind-body conversation, allows control of bodily processes that previously seemed involuntary (Kort, 1995), Miller's psychological research shows evidence for the possibility of being able to control processes such as negative emotions by means of a mind–body connection that can be understood as an involuntary result of learned processes and undeveloped tools becoming obstacles to peace building. In studies of quantum physics, a science that studies among its various subjects, subatomic particles, Sánchez and Márquez (2006) point to the mind as a creator through thoughts and feelings, expressing itself in a quantum field that makes one live a reality, even if one is not aware of the power to create that one has. Therefore this is called living in a dream (Corbera & Rubio, 2014).

But what is the relationship between the mind and the culture of peace? UNESCO (1992) suggests that it is in the minds of men that war begins and that is the place where it can be eradicated. Western education is considered to be oriented toward teaching children to memorize concepts, thus limiting their imagination. At this point, if the mind is indeed relevant, at what point in a human being's academic life is he or she provided with the tools to be at peace of mind? The question remains unanswered, because in Mexico, unless one studies for a degree in this area, there is no subject that focuses on reprogramming the subconscious to bring about behavioral changes.

Returning to the subject of silence, González (2011) points out the action of managing silences and provides some suggestions to generate positive habits in the process of active listening and silence, as described in the following:

- Timing silences allows people such as those with a blood profile to control their speech and develop the strength to listen.
- The habit of not being self-centered must be practiced.
- Quiet the inner voice that demands results.
- Go for positive postures.

Since students' childhood, teachers have often worn out their voices telling students to be silent, but with no success. Even in the most highly educated persons, participants continue to be silenced. It is difficult to control a group of people so that they remain silent. Where does the constant need of human beings to speak come from, even if they do not even understand what they are saying? Is it so much the egocentrism of one person who will not give time to another to be heard? Faced with these questions, it is pertinent to address the subject of calming the mind in order to achieve silence in speech. This learning should be taught by parents, who have the obligation to make their children understand the relevance of the subject starting in childhood, to encourage self-reflection in order to generate self-knowledge and to learn about self-knowledge and understanding the various benefits of learning to be silent.

Learning to be silent

In order for the role of the receiver to exist within a communication process, it is necessary to learn to be silent, since listening is the result of not speaking. This generates consequences such as balance in the actions of giving and receiving. As indicated by ancient cultures, balance could be a key point in daily coexistence. Considered as one of the first principles of the wise, King Solomon is a figure mentioned in some Ecclesiastical proverbs, catalogued as a man with the ability to be silent and listen. Time attributed to him the concept of Solomonic wisdom to qualify a wise, fair and intelligent decision to resolve conflicts (González, 2011).

There are circumstances in which it is suggested to remain silent and stay silent. Hernández (2008) recommends ten situations one should not establish a conversation with another person, as follows:

- When there is nothing important to say: this refers to not establishing empty and useless conversations; people who tend to engage in conversations of this type externalize deep deficiencies.
- When the right words cannot be found: silence is the best decision when, due to ignorance, fatigue or tiredness, there is no clarity of thought to understand the emotions that are being experienced.
- When there is no one to listen: when starting a conversation, the addressee is the stimulus; if there is no willingness of the receiving element, Hernández recommends keeping silent.
- When it is not the right time to speak: this refers to the appropriate context chosen to establish a conversation, where the circumstances, time and place are impertinent.
- When the facts speak: Hernández notes the relevance of silence as a way of communicating when an action does not require words.
- When others speak: it is suggested to establish turns when someone expresses himself or herself verbally; the receiver needs to establish an external and internal silence.
- When one is not serene: if there is no control of emotions, it is preferable to remain silent and remain calm, as there is a risk of establishing a kind of violence toward the other person.
- When you are surrounded by a lot of noise: it is preferable not to establish conversations if there are sounds that distort the message; the interference can act negatively within the communication process.

- When harmful words are approaching: Hernández refers to the power of words, from both a positive and a negative perspective. If they are not used in the right way, they represent a destructive tool in coexistence.
- When listeners do not pay attention or understand the words: when the addressee does not understand the language used, it is suggested not to elaborate speech, as it could be useless or annoying for others.

When to recognize the right time to speak out? Taking González (2015) as a reference, we describe some keys that indicate the right moment to speak or continue to remain silent:

> The first step is to learn to control impulses, which is the result of emotional, physical and spiritual skills. Depending on the temperament of the subject, it will be easier or more complex, but not impossible. It is a continuous exercise of self-observation that requires practice and time to act prudently; after exercising self-control, it is necessary to find the right moment to speak. To locate the right moment it is pertinent to sharpen the sensitivity and rhythm of the conversation. Listening until the person shows happiness for a period of time is key, and this time varies from subject to subject.
>
> (González, 2015)

A relevant guideline is to wait until a person has finished speaking, not to interrupt. When you have the opportunity to speak, do not just say anything. It is better to use convincing phrases. The idea of intervening is to contribute a productive idea. It is essential to remember that there are competitive people who will always want to be the center of attention. In that sense, it would be appropriate to act with reciprocity and not to listen to those who do not listen. Finally, González's recommendation is to wait, wait and wait. By letting others speak, it offers a chance to calm down; one can enjoy observing happiness in others by showing them appreciation, interest and respect for their life.

It is relevant to emphasize the identification of a toxic type of personality, that is, individuals who use friendship to discuss problems and situations, which only succeeds in wearing down the receiver. Drama is a constant in their daily lives and they do not act to change it, so they tend to adopt the role of victim of circumstances, with the aim of focusing attention on their problems. It is essential to consider that an interesting aspect of active listening also involves getting to know oneself and others, identifying and discerning the value of time given to a person. This subject is linked to the reciprocity of the parties. If there is no fairness, it is difficult to find a balance in the communication process. Both parties must contribute positive ideas and face the responsibility of living their lives.

Peace of mind

The second generation of peace studies, which deals with research on the subject of inner peace, reflects on the factor of silence and its relationship with peace of mind, indicating the close relationship that exists for the promotion of individual peace. A person has to learn to be in silence to have peace of mind. Human beings have not reached the level of being able to control their minds and this has been the cause of their suffering, so it is necessary to practice exercises that allow them to obtain an approach to mental control where they can manipulate their thoughts in such a way that they can transform the negative into happiness (Marizán, 2015). Marizán suggests that it is through meditation that one can access silence and find peace of mind; it is in that space between thought and thought that consciousness awakens and observes, not allowing the automatic brain to govern emotions of fear, conditioning and trauma, so it is at that moment when mental freedom is established.

The mind is considered a tyrant ruler that directs thoughts and actions in the way it wishes according to the mental programming of the subconscious, which is unknown. What Marizán points out is, first, to understand that thoughts can and should be controlled, because it is the self that should direct, not the mind. It is in this brief space between thought and thought that one experiences mental freedom and becomes aware that the human being himself can dominate and redirect what he feels or thinks.

Meditation, also known as mindfulness, was named and approved for use by the UK's National Institute for Clinical Excellence (NICE), and is employed to combat symptoms of stress such as depression, anger, chronic anxiety, addictions, insomnia, muscle tension and PMS, and has also been used to achieve greater concentration and efficiency in people (Puddicombe, 2010). Puddicombe considers that meditation is a skill and an experience; it requires regular practice to understand the benefits it can provide. The changes are subtle, intangible, increasing awareness, so it begins to generate a change in the way we perceive ourselves and others. Previously, it might have been thought that to approach the subject of meditation in science would be subjective and with a lack of studies to consider it a belief. Nowadays it has been given the name of mindfulness and is used to combat illnesses, as studies have shown that meditation benefits people's physical condition.

From the moment a person is born, they are in contact with their inner dialogue; it is part of the human condition and consciously or unconsciously, it is used frequently. There is no way to get rid of this dialogue, but if it can be calmed. People can work constantly and purposefully to foster a calm, focused and cooperative mind (Allen, 2013).

For Marizán (2015), the process of thinking in the human being occurs very fast. Between each thought one can have the perception that there are no spaces. Given this position modern science, through transpersonal psychology, has been able to prove that the thought process has pauses. At the point of change of thought in thought, there is a space generated, and it is the moment when silence appears. Marizán indicates that it is at that moment when there are no thoughts; it is when a kind of inner peace is noticed. There is no mental movement because there is a space for mental peace. This space can have a duration of a millisecond or a microsecond, and the longer the silence is maintained, the more mental peace a person can have.

By constantly practicing mindfulness, a person can achieve interesting changes in their daily life and their relationship with others, mainly in their behavior, which will become calmer, more relaxed and will favor self-control. It is for this reason that peace of mind is so important in the subject of the culture of peace. Without its practice, it is difficult to have a peaceful coexistence within a marriage or any interpersonal relationship. Not only is the lack of peace of mind considered to generate a lack of control, but it also influences the individual's ability to heed and understand a message.

Attention and understanding (mindfulness)

The second indicator of active listening is attention and understanding. This section describes definitions of the origin and concept, providing evidence of the nonverbal communication signals emitted by the body unconsciously, to express when attention and understanding are present in situations or people.

The key to any interpretation is to listen carefully. According to experts, it is required to attach meaning to the information received. Once interpreted, understanding proceeds, defined as getting a simple idea of things (Gonzalez, 2011). Kabat-Zinn (2005, as cited in Siegel, 2012) defines mindfulness as a total focus of attention in each moment of daily life without carrying out judgments, expectations or conceived ideas. It arises from practicing contemplation, focusing the waking mind on things as they are in order to be continuously living in the present. For Pavón (2015), attention can be understood as a broad perceptive power of the mind and senses, making it a transcendent factor in the development of people's cognitive potential.

According to Goleman (2013), the word attention comes from the Latin word *attendere*, which means to tend toward; it constitutes a mental value. On the other hand, although its study is little recognized, it has a relevant influence on the way we act in life. Cognitive science has developed the study of attention and its variables, such as: concentration, selective attention, open awareness, management and supervision of mental operations, executive control directing attention to the interior.

It seems that there is still a lot to be explored in the field of attention. It is interesting to study consciousness; the process of internalization of the self; the factors that cause some people to be inclined toward the practice of techniques that allow them to direct their attention toward the mind; and the reasons why others ignore it.

Currently, the science of attention has expanded and has concluded that it is a person's attentional skills that determine the level of performance in any activity. If a subject's attentional skills are deficient, the work performed will also be deficient; however, if they maintain adequate attention, the function can be excellent (Goleman, 2013). Goleman indicates that the existence of attention on the part of the individual lies in the functioning of many mental operations, among the main ones are: understanding, possessing self-knowledge, reading other people's emotions, establishing healthy interpersonal relationships, learning and using memory. The results of studies in neuroscience indicate that attention is comparable to a muscle; to the extent that it is exercised it develops. On the contrary, if it is not used, it will be weakened; selective attention is the neuronal capacity to concentrate in the midst of noise, ignoring any other center of attention and focusing interest on what is selected (Goleman, 2013).

Today, living in a world of technology, it is interesting to observe the attention given to people. The generation of 20 years ago did not have such innovative distractors as today. As Goleman mentions, attention represents a relevant value for well-being. Could a lack of attention trigger unhealthy coexistence behaviors?

A study by the *CyberPsychology & Behavior* journal indicates that the social network Facebook has generated around 28 million separations worldwide. This is due to the attention and time spent on social networks, which causes 95 percent of users to look for their ex-partners, causing encounters, infidelities and breakups (El País, 2013).

Goleman (2013) indicates that attention regulates emotion, so in moments of lack of control, the self-control technique of distraction is used, which focuses attention to another point in order to relax the amygdala, thus decreasing the intensity of the negative emotion and allowing the emotions to level out. Goleman points out the existence of two types of distractions: sensory and emotional. The simplest are the sensory and they are related to bodily sensations, for example, the fluorescent color of the title of a book,

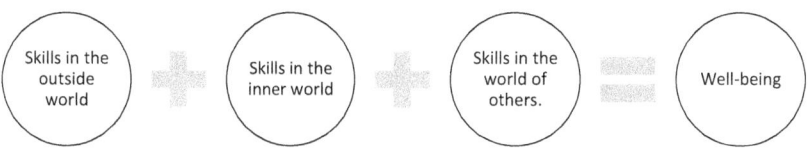

Figure 3.3 Areas for proper living.
Source: Own elaboration based on Goleman (2013).

while the emotional distractors are of great influence, preventing one from focusing attention on something or someone.

This type of technique pointed out by Goleman is widely used in childhood, where the topic is changed or the child is shown an eye-catching distractor or an object that manages to remove attention from a topic that is causing a negative emotion. In this sense, the adult can use this technique to avoid obsessing with thoughts or actions that cause negative emotions and may generate violent behaviors.

Figure 3.3 shows a series of skills that Goleman (2013) identifies in order to live adequately. It describes those related to the external world, which refer to survival; skills in the internal world, which are related to the ability to regulate and self-control thoughts and emotions; and skills with others, in which components such as active listening, frustration tolerance and assertive language, relevant for peaceful coexistence, are perceived.

Continuing with the topic of empathy, authors such as Balart (2013) point out that it is an emotional competence that is achieved at an intellectual level, active listening at an emotional level, and understanding and assertiveness at a behavioral level. Empathy, defined as a tool for connecting with others, aims to understand the feelings, needs and problems that others have, putting oneself in the other person's place in order to understand them. Moya-Albiol (2014, as cited in Buelga, 2014) stresses that empathizing means learning to take the other person's place by understanding their mind and emotions, with a clearer vision of the situation since the emotional discomfort that the sender expresses is not experienced. Moya-Albiol indicates that empathy reinforces values such as tolerance, respect, happiness, solidarity, and favoring a healthy coexistence between people, decreasing the appearance of violent behavior in the individual, and achieving an openness toward reciprocal dialogue that allows the peaceful resolution of conflicts.

Understanding is an attitude that arises from complete and open attention to understand the feelings and needs of the other. It implies compassion and action, because it suggests or proposes to establish means, connections or behaviors that favor the other. Moya-Albiol indicates that people who in their childhood have been accepted, loved and cared for have a greater capacity to understand others. Understanding does not imply agreeing with what the sender expresses; rather, it means listening without judging, empathizing and respecting their point of view (Balart, 2013).

What Balart mentions about the relevance of the topic of people's childhood, is something that parents seem to be unaware of. Nowadays, a great number of distractions exist, not to mention work-related issues that take the family away from coexistence, which generates moments of attention, understanding and care for the child, suggesting that it is difficult for a child neglected by his or her parents to generate listening skills toward others in his or her adult life.

In order to understand, it is necessary to participate, to have an intention, to ask the other to confirm or correct what has been understood. This is what participatory understanding refers to. Grondin (2008, as cited in Montes, 2013) asserts that the process of understanding lies in recreating in oneself the feeling that someone else has experienced. Regarding this topic, a genuine interest in the other or the situation is an indispensable requirement. The understanding that one has about the message sent by the sender is related to a real affection toward the individual, affection that generates patience and that in its absence makes the process of understanding complex, due to the inability to reflect, which requires time and participation.

Approaching the topic of attention and understanding lies in presenting indicators of nonverbal communication, such as movements, facial expressions, accentuations and actions with the body that indicate concentration on what someone else is expressing or, on the contrary, a lack of interest in the conversation. Body language or nonverbal language has the same meaning, as those are signals and gestures that the body uses to communicate. Interestingly, more accurate information is obtained about the movements that are made than what a person speaks, because body language indicates an emotional intention (Arbeláez, 2014). Arbeláez points out that studies indicate that when interacting with someone or something, the body is the first to manifest and communicate. After milliseconds, the person becomes aware of what they are experiencing, finally identifying the sensation lucidly and announcing it verbally.

The voluntary and involuntary bodily signals emitted by the body to communicate something are called "tells", a term in English. There are three categories of tells: kinesthetic, paralinguistic and proxemic. Taking Arbeláez (2014) as a reference, kinesthetic tells are described as referring to the study of gestures, body posture and facial expressions made by the body.

- **Gestures:** are divided into two types: emplomas and illustrators. The first have their own meaning, for example, moving the head from one side to the other, indicating a no response, whereas illustrators have no meaning, for example, pointing a finger to indicate a place.
- **Body posture:** this is the predisposition one has when interacting with someone else. There are open and closed postures, which depend on the angle at which people choose to sit. An example of a closed posture is sitting in front of someone else. This type of behavior indicates competition, while sitting to a person's side is done because both people intend to collaborate.
- **Facial expression:** studies have detected more than 3,000 micro gestures made by the face, but there are six primary facial expressions: joy, sadness, disgust, anger, astonishment and fear.

For other authors, such as Domínguez (2009), there are not only three tells but also four currently recognized nonverbal communication systems. Taking Domínguez as a reference, kinesthetic and paralanguage tells, primary, as well as proxemics and tactesics tells, secondary, are described.

Paralinguistic is a science that deals with the study of voice qualities—intensity, pitch, timbre, tempo and rhythm; qualifiers—type of voice and control according to the context; differentiators—laughing, crying, yawning, sneezing and alternating; and noise in communication, as well as pauses and silences in a communication process. Pauses and silences are a relevant mechanism in the process of discourse or conversation, exerting nuance and emphasis in each occurrence. With regard to silences, they can corroborate statements, indicate a correction or be made in response to a question.

Proxemics is the science that deals with the study of nonverbal behavior related to the organization of space. Space is classified into two categories: physical or territorial space, and personal or psychological space. The first refers to the study of the behavior generated by the physical movement that generates a space between one country or elsewhere. The second is the space delimited by human beings when they are in a process of communication with someone else, which according to Edwuart Hall, is not the result of their will but of their unconscious. Hall made a classification of distances, among which are from physical contact to 45cm; from 40cm to 1.20 m—distance used between friends; from 1.20 to 2.70 m—social distance between strangers; and more than 2.70 m—the public distance for official conversations.

Tactesics studies everything related to the contact that the human body makes in its interaction with someone else: the frequency, intensity, context and what is considered most relevant to the final objective with which the interactions are carried out.

Little relevance and diffusion are given to studies related to the science of paralinguistics, to teach about the appropriate tone of voice to engage in conversations according to the person with whom one is interacting. Talking to acquaintances and colleagues is different from talking between a couple; a special tone of voice is required that favors harmonious coexistence. Simple actions such as using a tone of voice with tenderness or gentleness could be the ideal way to get the attention of the receiver and facilitate the understanding of the message. This type of behavior could change an emotional state that reactivates listening and in turn spreads a chain of trust that generates peaceful approaches in the couple.

To conclude the chapter, we return to the topic of the mind, which is intended to be approached seriously, mainly in the meditation or mindfulness techniques mentioned above, emphasizing that it is a matter for science to attend to research related to the benefit of society in order to improve its quality of life. If studies have shown the benefits of calming the mind and UNESCO has pointed it out as the solution to war, it is nevertheless still a pending and forgotten task for education, family and society to attend to mental control and the learning of techniques that allow us to calm our thoughts.

To conclude, it is essential to reiterate the positive consequences of feeling listened to. On an emotional level, being listened to is related to the respect, love, attention and care offered to someone else. If self-esteem is an indispensable element for the selection of assertive communication styles, active listening needs to be addressed and taught as a matter of urgency.

Reflection questions

1. What are the five profiles of temperament and level of listening that human beings can adopt?
2. Describe the difference between hearing and listening.
3. What are the fundamental rules for good listening?
4. What are some negative habits that block listening?
5. What would be the relationship or common thread between listening and the culture of peace?
6. What are the different types of listening?
7. What is active listening?
8. Name some benefits of active listening.
9. What is silence?
10. What is mindfulness?

References

Allen, M. (2013). *Cómo Callar Su Mente: Relájese y Silencie la Voz de su Mente Hoy*. CreateSpace Independent Publishing Platform.

Arbeláez, J. (2014). *Súper Lenguaje Corporal.* Cuidad de México: Mente Lateral.

Balart Gritti, M. J. (mayo de 2013). *La empatia: la clave para conectar con los demás.* Recuperado el 9 de febrero de 2016, de Observatorio de recursos humanos y relaciones laborales: www.gref.org/nuevo/articulos/art_250513.pdf

Buelga, S. (julio–diciembre de 2014). *La empatia:entenderla para entender a los demás.* Recuperado el 9 de marzo de 2016, de Pensamiento Psicológico: http://revistas.javerianacali.edu.co/index.php/pensamientopsicologico/article/view/941

Cala, I. (2013). *El poder de escuchar*. New York: Penguin Press.

Codina Jiménez, A. (septiembre–octubre de 2004). *Saber escuchar. Un intangible valioso.* Recuperado el 18 de noviembre de 2014, de Intangible Capital: www.redalyc.org/pdf/549/54900303.pdf

Corbera, E., & Rubio, R. (2014). *Visión Cuántica del Transgerenacional.* Barcelona: El grano de mostaza.

Domínguez Lázaro, M. (noviembre–enero de 2009). *La Importancia de la Comunicación No Verbal en el Desarrollo Cultural de las Sociedades.* Recuperado el 10 de marzo de 2016, de Razón y Palabra: www.redalyc.org/pdf/1995/199520478047.pdf

El País. (31 de marzo de 2013). *Estudios revelan que Facebook ha provocado 28 millones de divorcios.* Recuperado el octubre de 2016, de El País: www.elpais.com.co/elpais/internacional/noticias/estudios-revelan-facebook-ha-provocado-28-millones-divorcios

García Román, M. (2015). *Manual del Silencio. Ejercicios simples para una mente en paz.* Kindle Edition: Amazon Digital Services.

Goleman, D. (2013). *Focus. Desarrollar la atención para alcanzar la excelencia.* Barcelona: Kairós.

González A., S. (2011). *Habilidades de comunicación y escucha: Empatía + alto nivel + resultados.* Nashville, TN: Graciela Lellí.

González A., S. (2015). *El ABC de la comunicación afectiva: hablada, escrita, escuchada.* Nashville: Grupo Nelson.

Hernández Guerrero, J. (2008). *El arte de callar.* Cádiz: Diputación Provincial de Cádiz.

Hérnando Gómez, Á., Aguaded Gómez, I., & Pérez Rodríguez, A. (2011). *Técnicas de comunicación creativas en el aula:escucha activa, el arte de la pregunta, la gestión de los silencios.* Recuperado el 24 de febrero de 2016, de Educación y Futuro: http://rabida.uhu.es/dspace/bitstream/handle/10272/6311/Tecnicas_de_comunicacion_creativa.pdf?sequence=2

Kort, F. (1995). *Interacción mente-cuerpo.* Recuperado el 28 de septiembre de 2014, de Revista Latinoamericana de Psicología: www.redalyc.org/pdf/805/80527307.pdf

McEntee de Madero, E., & Férnandez, A. (1993). *Comunicación oral: el arte y la ciencia de hablar en público.* Cuidad de México: Alhambra Mexicana, S.A. de C.V.

Maldonado Willman, H. (1998). *Manual de comunicación oral.* Cuidad de México: Longman de México Editores, S.A. de C.V.

Marizán, J. (2015). *El espacio entre dos pensamientos: Meditación en Silencio.* CreateSpace Independent Publishing Platform.

Montes Sosa, G. (enero–junio de 2013). *Entender, Comprender, Interpretar.* Recuperado el 9 de marzo de 2016, de Enseñanza e Investigación en Psicología: www.cneip.org/documentos/revista/181/13.pdf

Muñoz Hernán, Y., Ramos Pérez, M. E., & Romera, C. (noviembre de 2012). *Guía para el Diálogo y la Resolución de los Conflictos Cotidianos*. Recuperado el 9 de marzo de 2016, de Giza Eskubideak Derechos Humanos: www.ceapa.es/content/gu%C3%ADa-para-el-di%C3%A1logo-y-la-resoluci%C3%B3n-de-conflictos-cotidiano-diputaci%C3%B3n-foral-de-guip%C3%BAzcoa

Ortiz Crespo, R. (2007). *Aprender a Escucha. Cómo Desarrollar la Capacidad de la Escucha Activa*. Lulu.com.

Pavón, M. A. (2015). *El Pode Curativo de la Atención*. CreateSpace Independent Publishing Platform.

Polaino-Lorente, A. (2008). *Aprender a Escuchar*. Recuperado el 17 de marzo de 2016, de CEU Biblioteca: http://dspace.ceu.es/bitstream/10637/5264/1/Libro.pdf

Puddicombe, A. (2010). *Mindfulness Atención Plena. Haz espacio en tu mente*. Madrid: EDAF.

Redorta, J. (2006). *Cómo analizar los conflictos: la tipologia de conflictos como herramienta de mediación*. Barcelona: PAIDOS IBERICA.

Sánchez Medina, G., & Márquez Díaz, J. (2006). *Revista Colombiana de Psiquiatría*. Recuperado el 28 de septiembre de 2014, de El pensamiento cuántico. Una propuesta teórica: www.redalyc.org/pdf/806/80635308.pdf

Santibáñez Velilla, J. (2015). *Aprender juntos. La escucha activa del otro. Comunicación verbal y comunicación no verbal entre un tutor y un alumno*. Recuperado el 26 de febrero de 2016, de REIRE: revista d'innovació i recerca en educació: https://dialnet.unirioja.es/servlet/articulo?codigo=5187062

Satir, V. (2015). *Ejercicios para la Comunicación Humana*. Cuidad de México: Pax.

Serrano-Puche, J. (2015). Emociones en el uso de la tecnología: Un análisis de las investigaciones sobre teléfonos móviles. Observatorio OSB Journal, 101–12.

Siegel, D. (2012). *Mindfulness y Psicoterapia*. Barcelona: Paidós Ibérica.

UNESCO. (1992). *UNESCO*. Recuperado el 23 de septiembre de 2014, de El Manifiesto de Sevilla sobre Violencia: http://unesdoc.unesco.org/images/0009/000943/094314so.pdf

Chapter 4

Skill 3
Tolerance to frustration

Low frustration tolerance and violence

First, it is relevant to understand when addressing the topic of FT, the individual meaning of these two words that in themselves have their own definition. Tolerance, according to the dictionary of the Royal Spanish Academy (2016), can be defined in various ways: the action of tolerating, respect for ideas, recognition, a right. In a word, it could be defined as enduring.

With regard to frustration, studies on the topic date back to the 1950s (Santiago, 2001). Regarding its definition, Teruel (2015) points out that it is the result of a desire that has not been realized. For Hurtado, De la Cruz and Robles (2015), it is a force intended for the realization of a specific aspect, but when it is not carried out, when it remains static without achieving the desired objective, that force that was focused to carry out something unfulfilled must be removed in order not to generate any action, behavior or negative situation.

When a desire, goal or need is not fulfilled, frustration is generated in adults and children, triggering a series of emotions such as sadness, anxiety, anger and anguish. Each person experiences a different type of frustration. Constructing a definition of FT based on what Hurtado, De la Cruz and Robles mention, it can be synthesized as the action of enduring an unfulfilled desire or goal. By possessing this component, one perceives a regulation and transformation of different types of emotions that would favor dialogue and non-violent coexistence with other people.

In this sense, frustration is not only exclusive to human beings, since according to studies on frustration in animals, they learn to establish expectations about different events to which they are continuously exposed, and through that a current or future behavior is developed. For Flaherty (1996, as cited in Ruetti & Justel, 2010), failure to meet expectations can trigger emotions such as: frustration, disappointment or euphoria. The type of behavior that arises when an expectation is not met in both humans and animals is frustration, so the emotion is perceived with a natural essence, and other living beings also experience it. Thus, it is not intended to inhibit frustration in people but rather an acceptance and transformation.

According to studies, a person in a situation of frustration can respond in three ways: to oneself, to others, to the situation. Against oneself: the individual may start to attack him- or herself with negative thoughts, devaluing him- or herself and becoming unmotivated (Santiago Lopezó, 2001). Santiago Lopezó suggests that one responds with blaming behaviors toward others, which can trigger anger, hostility, arguments, fights and physical aggression. Finally, the response against the situation manifests itself in flight or escape reactions through excessive shopping, alcohol, drugs and more.

Pappini, Wood, Daniel and Norris (2006, as cited in Ruetti & Justel, 2010) indicate that the results of frustration in animals produce changes in their behavior, with crying, avoidance and escape responses, as well as aggressive reactions toward other animals and their environment. Among the consequences indicated by studies on the aggressive behavior of animals in their environment, it is preciscly what needs to be curbed in people.

Aggressive behavior triggered by an unfulfilled event, it is perceived, could be a permeable avenue for emotional violence within the marriage.

In order to understand the cause of violent behavior in humans, taking Amarista (2008) as a reference, the four possible origins and nature of this type of behavior are described:

1. The Instinctive: its main exponent was Freud; his philosophy proposes that the human being is aggressive from birth.
2. Frustration: J. Delay and P. Pichot (1996) suggest that violence is based on activating an impulse developed through a previous situation of frustration, which prevents the fulfillment of a goal,

event and so forth. All frustration generates aggression and all aggression responds to a frustrating event.
3. Acquired: For Montagu (1968, cited in Amarista, 2008), violent or aggressive behavior is learned through social factors. Montagu observes that if a child is satisfied in his biological needs, feels loved and develops less frustration, he will never opt for aggressive behavior.
4. Amarista explains aggressive behavior as an innate and acquired result of society.

As shown in Figure 4.1, the origin of violence is not only described from Sigmund Freud's instinctive cause: frustration, acquired and mixed. There is also another classification that conceives the idea that this type of behavior could be biological, transmitted by genetic information or by brain and endocrine problems.

Freud, Delay, Pichot and Montagu, as presented here, stressed two concepts: aggression and violence, so it is necessary to understand whether the definitions indicate similarities, or whether different concepts are addressed. In this regard, the Royal Spanish Academy (2016b; RAE) indicates that a violent person is somebody who reacts with force and impetus, allowing themselves to be carried away by anger, while the aggressive person tends to disrespect, offend and provoke others (Real Academia Española, 2016a). Both are behaviors that aggravate others or the person him- or herself. The difference lies in the fact that an aggressive person is one who has a predisposition, while a violent person only reacts. These

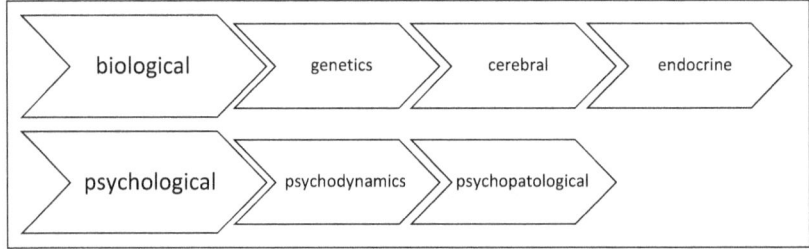

Figure 4.1 Causes of violent behavior.
Source: Own elaboration based in Amarista (2008).

are understood as levels, where being aggressive might be easier to handle compared to the violent subject; however, both cases require attention and transformation.

From a psychological perspective, the approach followed in this book continues Amarista's (2008) thinking to explain the foundations of the five psychodynamic causes of aggression: identification, imitation, frustration, instinctual drives and inner control deficits.

In identification, the individual adopts the aggressive behaviors of someone else; in imitation, he or she adheres to a model and acts the same as the selected personality. In frustration, Dollard and Miller (1932, as cited in Amatista, 2008) proposed the frustration–aggression hypothesis, in which they mention the constant relationship that exists between a frustrating event and aggressive behavior. The relationship between frustration and violence is evident in the studies presented, so proposing the FT component is supported by the diversity of psychodynamic causes. To investigate this topic further, it is necessary to know what frustration–aggression theory has to say about it.

An approach to frustration–aggression theory

According to Worchel (2002, as cited in Chapi, 2012), there are four theories from a psychological perspective that explain human aggression: instinct theory, neurobiological theory, frustration–aggression theory and social learning theory. In this section, an approach to the frustration–aggression theory is made.

Taking Chapi (2012) as a reference, a description of the sources and main points addressed by the theory is given. The general idea suggests frustration as the cause of aggressive behavior. In contrast, research by Berkowitz (as cited in Chapi, 2012) does not support this hypothesis and points out that frustration is not always reacted to with violence, as it can be stimulated by the environmental context. For Symonds (as cited in Chapi, 2012), the sources of frustration are the following:

- Restriction of exploratory behavior: this occurs when the infant begins to put objects in his mouth and his parents block this behavior, which begins to generate frustration in the infant.

- Restriction of the first sexual experiences: this occurs when the infant experiments with touching certain areas of his or her body, which is pleasurable, and the parents forcefully prevent this type of behavior.
- Rivalries within the family: the birth of someone else in the family generates interest in the new member, causing frustration in the other siblings.
- Early feeding frustrations: studies show that infants who have been fed for short periods of time in infancy are frustrated.
- Loss of protection: this is generated by the prolonged absence of the infant's parents, responding to behaviors of insecurity and lack of protection.
- Formation of cleanliness habits: continuous toilet and sphincter control education leads to frustration in childhood.
- Decreased dependence on parents: this refers to when parents force the child to carry out activities independently, using his or her own resources.
- Frustrations at school: the pressure to perform well academically, to control one's temperament, generates tension and frustration in the child.
- Frustrations in adolescence: the adjustment of the adolescent to maturity, responsibility and socializing with the opposite sex generates frustration in young people.
- Adult frustrations: economic, professional and social needs.

When reflecting on the sources of frustration pointed out by the theory, the impossibility of eliminating all the situations of frustration in which the subject develops throughout his life is evident, because many circumstances are not within his control and are the result of external factors. There is a relationship between the research problem of individual deprivation and the theories of frustration–aggression and social learning. Both address a deficiency in components that are not developed in the subject from an early age; on the one hand, self-control and from the family perspective as an example of imitation and identification, so it is proposed the continuous exercise of learning techniques to control frustration, in which there is a recognition of the emotion and channeling of that force in a positive way, with the aim of developing tools of tolerance in their adult life.

How to be tolerant of frustration

For some authors, interpersonal relationships are based on emotional intelligence (EI). Acquiring EI requires certain skills such as awareness of emotions, feelings and needs, and this type of state allows maintaining constructive and satisfying relationships. The management of stressful situations is one of those skills that socially and emotionally define a person with FT (Oliva et al., 2011).

According to Hurtado and Robles (2010), it is essential to develop strategies such as cultivating a positive attitude and a culture of effort, doing things by oneself, not letting anger dominate the situation, setting realistic goals and turning the problematic situation into a learning process.

For Teruel (2015), self-observation can be a tool for people suffering from frustration, as focusing attention on the thoughts of everyday life will help people recognize true desires and needs. Another escape valve for the emergence of frustration suggests accepting what has happened and rethinking new actions, doing swimming activities and experiencing sexual pleasure, simple five-minute exercises for daily observation of predominant emotions and behaviors, could make a significant difference in the development of FT, due to the process of self-observation, which promotes reflection and analysis of situations for mental flexibility.

Teruel's point of view in suggesting aquatic activities as an option to remove the repressed force that causes frustration seems interesting, since in Mexico the population is distinguished by the opposite. Statistics show that 58.2% of women and 41.8% of men do not engage in any type of physical activity (INEGI, 2015).

The study indicates that of those who are physically active, the majority go to private gyms in the morning. The routine they follow is not specified, but it is inferred that only a minority have access to frequent aquatic activity, an action that, according to Tereul, could combat frustration.

Another alternative is frustration therapy. Santiago (2001) indicates the stages through which it is integrated:

1. Reflection on common frustration response behaviors: the common type of response to frustration is identified and a reflection on the consequences of responding in this way is carried out.
2. Coping: training in coping responses is carried out. When the subject is aware of his or her negative behavior, he or she proposes alternative solutions.
3. Cooling down: it is suggested that the subject adopt the technique of distancing him- or herself from the problem, in order to be able to think more clearly and calm down.
4. Internal coherence between cognitive schemes, principles or values and behaviors to promote self-direction: studies indicate that people with greater emotional instability remain in the role of victims. Through questions and schemes, the aim is to promote self-knowledge, self-acceptance, self-esteem and coherence between principles and behaviors.

Regarding treatments to resolve psychological causes, Amarista (2008) indicates that among the studies to reduce aggressiveness in subjects are: individual psychotherapy, psychodrama, psychoanalysis, occupational therapy and music therapy. For their part, other authors observe that it is in childhood, when adversities can help a person develop more strategies to overcome future setbacks more easily in adult life. Acting on the causes of identification, imitation, drive, frustration and internal control could be effective in reducing aggression in the individual (Torres & Baillés, 2014).

Since the twentieth century, attempts have been made to reduce violence in the world but to no avail, from the creation of the Convention of World Citizens to a scientist's idea of pouring lithium salts into the aqueducts of large cities to reduce violence in individuals (Amarista, 2008). Some of the solutions proposed by authors are sympathetic. What is certain, however, is the urgency to address and prevent violent or aggressive behavior, which is a topic that requires deep introspection and the real need to effect change in one's relationship with oneself and others.

Without a genuine intention for transformation, it is difficult for individuals to begin to manage the emotions that cause them to react negatively. Another option is the study of transgenerational and systems theory, which could be an alternative solution to finding the basis for aggressive behavior and lack of control in stressful situations and a negative disposition. Searching through the family unconscious for the repetition of violent scenarios is an interesting area for exploring and addressing causes that are not easily perceived.

Understanding stress

Having addressed the topic of FT in a general way, it is pertinent to delve into the first of its indicators: stress management. The aim is to clearly understand its definition from a psychological perspective, the types of stress, its typology and how to manage it. The first questions that come to mind are: What is stress? Is it an emotion? Is it the daily feeling of irritability, of annoyance? Can stress lead a person to respond with or to adopt violent behavior in daily relationships, in this specific case with a partner? Would stress management in any way promote a culture of peace within the marriage?

To answer these questions, it is necessary to know what some authors and studies indicate. The word "stress" comes from the Latin word *stringere*, which means to squeeze, oppress, bind. It can also be understood as a feeling of abandonment, helplessness and loneliness. It is understood as a physical or psychological burden on a living organism, also called a syndrome that manifests itself in the face of an event (Maroto, 2015). Regarding its definition, the word stress was first used by the physician and physiologist Hans Selye, who pointed out that stress was not a disease but a useful and efficient physiological response that can be harmful in certain circumstances (Torres & Baillés, 2014). For WHO (2004), stress can be caused by problems at home or work-related issues. It is caused on the one hand, by an imbalance between the demands placed on the subject, and on the other, by their knowledge or lack thereof.

In the face of a threatening response, the individual may feel stress only if their beliefs make them think that it is an uncontrollable or unpredictable threat. Stress will depend on whether the person has the perception that they will not be able to handle the situation, of an inability to cope (Torres & Baillés, 2014). In Mexico, the Instituto de Seguridad y Servicios Sociales de los Trabajadores del Estado (Institute of Security and Social Services for State Workers) (2016) indicates that stress is an internal mental state of tension produced by a stressor stimulus, which can be an event, person or object, producing a physiological and psychological response.

Oppression, imbalance, physiological response, internal state and perception according to the belief system are some of the concepts defined by various authors. The term "mental state" most accurately integrates the concept of stress. It is considered that stress cannot be an emotion, because it is in turn composed of emotions; therefore, it is a mental state that can be entered and exited at any time, producing different responses. The state varies from person to person because the belief system is different in each subject. Stress is perceived to be related to the subjects' self-esteem.

When individuals find themselves in stressful situations, they generate a variety of behaviors that are easily detectable. Taking Torres and Baillés (2014) as a reference, they describe some of the symptoms suffered by people who continuously present periods of recurrent stress, including the following:

- They are irritable, easily frustrated, constantly express complaints.
- Increased sensitivity arises; they may start to cry over ordinary situations.
- They show no sense of humor and they remain in a state of reserve.
- A loss of interest in everyday activities is triggered.
- They smoke and drink alcohol or coffee in excess.
- They grind their teeth when sleeping.
- They experience a loss of weight or appetite and excessive colds.
- They are constantly worrying, have trouble concentrating, have difficulty making decisions and have constant negative thoughts.

There exists the ability to react in different ways to situations of threat or tension. Some people have the ability to adapt to continuous or repetitive stress and manage to solve it more easily than others. When a case corresponds to subjects who do not have this tool, in the presence of external stimuli the results are emotional, mental changes or psychosomatic syndromes (Maroto, 2015). It is established that the more complications that have arisen in the initial stages of life, the more likely it is that in adulthood these individuals will have the ability to know how to manage better states of frustration or irritability, since the individual was previously subjected to unpleasant situations that they managed to overcome.

Stress is considered the disease of the twenty-first century because it affects a large number of people around the world. Stress not only causes irregular behaviors but, according to Jean Benjamin Stora, it can also cause symptoms such as gastric ulcers, constipation, diarrhea, arthritis, diabetes, colitis, fatigue states and migraines (Maroto, 2015). The way of reacting to stress varies from person to person, as mentioned above. According to Meichenbaum and Turkb (1972, as cited in Regional Institute for Occupational Safety and Health, 2011), there are three types of people with different types of stress behaviors:

- Self-referential individuals: people of this type constantly pay attention only to the negative, do not solve anything and are in a never-ending cycle.
- Self-efficient individuals: these individuals focus on the solution, evaluate and resolve. Their attention is on solving a problem.
- Individuals in denial: they deny the existence of a problem, avoid and never solve anything.

The type of person who is most aligned with the culture of peace are self-effective, efficient personalities, with a flexible mentality that makes it possible to find alternative solutions to stress and to escape quickly from this state of mind.

Maroto (2015) finds that there are three levels of stress:

> The first stage is called alarm. It is characterized by an increased level of adrenaline in the body, and breathing becomes rapid and the heart rate increases. This alarm awakens the body to

any kind of action. The behavior can be unpredictable. The resistance stage is where the person reacts to the situation and deals with it. In this sense each person reacts in a different way, whether by expressing themselves, paralyzing themselves or tensing their voice. In the last stage, called exhaustion, there is an excess of tension in the person who does not express him- or herself because of an erroneous idea about not generating conflict. The body needs to release this tension, which can manifest itself in anxiety crises, panic or hysteria attacks.

It is necessary to recognize the alarm stage immediately in order to carry out some type of regulation and not to adopt violent behavior. It is the primary phase of stress that requires continuous action, such as deep breathing, in order to establish a connection between what the body experiences and the continuous thoughts, so that the subject does not react impulsively but in a conscious way.

To assess the levels of stress that a person has, Maroto (2015) suggests using the Holmes-Rahe scale, in which a value is mentioned depending on the event that is arising in the a person's daily life. For example, a change in the economic situation generates 38 points of stress; an increase in arguments between the couple 35; divorce 73; marital separation 65; death of a spouse or a child 100 points. The scale indicates that if the sum of the score is less than 150 units, there is a 30 percent chance of suffering health problems; if the total is 300 units the chances increase to 50%. Scoring more than 300 units in the total score indicates that the person has an 80% chance that their health will be severely affected.

The emotions of stress

Stress is conceptualized as a mental state, which varies in its typology depending on the stressor that provokes it: it can be emotional, occupational and so on. It is responsible for producing emotions such as anger, anxiety and depression, which are categorized as the three emotions of stress (Miller et al., 1994). Emotions and the human being have been a topic reviewed by several authors. Studies and investigations have been carried out to understand their taxonomy, their function, and their relationship with the brain and the chemical substances that trigger a series of physical reactions that harm or benefit the individual.

To clarify the definition of emotion, Redorta, Obiols and Bisquerra (2006) note that it is the emotional state of a person that determines the way he or she perceives the world; therefore, an emotion is produced in the following way:

1. Sensory information reaches the emotional centers of the brain.
2. As a consequence, there is a neurophysiological response.
3. The brain interprets the information and prepares the organism to respond.

In synthesis, in the process of emotional experience, when an unexpected event occurs, the brain immediately, according to the system it has, sends a response that is expressed on a neurophysiological, behavioral and cognitive level. Among the responses, the neurophysiological response, as Redorta, Obiols and Bisquerra point out, represents the reaction that the nervous system manifests in the body: producing tachycardia, sweating and so forth. As for the behavioral response, it is the way in which the subject proceeds or acts in response to the emotion. Finally, the cognitive response generates some kind of knowledge.

The appraisal process can have several phases: the primary phase that relates the relevance of the event; the appraisal phase, which is very fast, in which it is identified whether the event is positive or negative and an emotion is generated; the secondary phase, which involves personal resources such as self-esteem to cope with the event (Redorta et al., 2006). According to what Redorta et al. mention, the appraisal system can be interpreted as the belief system, or the filter that a situation has to go through, and according to the ideas that the individual possesses, it will be qualified. It is the tools available to the person that will favor a positive action in the situation.

In the face of a deficit of the tools that favor positive action in a marriage, it is useful to intervene in the process of creating emotion, strengthening the individual's system of practices and peace components for the improvement of coexistence.

The various types of responses that an emotion can cause a person to experience were mentioned earlier. In the discipline of psychology, emotion is defined as a multidimensional experience with at least three response systems. Piqueras Rodríguez et al. (2009) describe the types, as shown below:

1. Cognitive/subjective: corresponds to a response at the level of thinking or interpretation.
2. Behavioral/expressive: refers to the expression of emotions.
3. Physiological/adaptive: points to the arousal of the organism as a response mechanism.

In this way, in order to understand emotions, it is necessary to pay attention to the response systems, in which there is no certain synchrony in the moment when the response manifests itself. At the psychological level, an individual can react in at least three different ways to an emotion, which can be mental, expressive and produce reactions in the organism.

Other authors, such as Chóliz (n.d., as cited in Piqueras Rodríguez et al., 2009), refer to emotions as being the cause of a series of pleasant or unpleasant sensations and can be regularly intense. In this sense, unpleasant emotions are reviewed, which are those that could block a peaceful reaction in human beings.

At this point, according to Piqueras Rodríguez et al., emotions can be positive or negative. They have various forms of response, which produce favorable or unfavorable sensations depending on their intensity, but what are the negative emotions that are harmful to the individual? Some research indicates that fear, sadness, anger and disgust are emotional states that, when intense, negatively affect people's quality of life, becoming an important risk factor for contracting diseases (Piqueras Rodríguez et al., 2009).

For the psychiatric sciences, negative emotions are: anxiety, anger, sadness or depression. Sometimes there are pathological reactions in certain individuals due to mismatches in frequency or intensity. When such a mismatch occurs, a health disorder can also occur, both mental—anxiety disorder, major depression and so on—and physical (Cano & Miguel, 2001).

From a philosophical perspective, the study of negative emotions has been classified into three roots: anger, grief and fear, each of which can trigger ramifications such as sadness, hatred, fear, anxiety, depression, worry and stress, to name a few (Menéndez, 2008). If we compare studies from psychological, psychiatric and philosophical thought, anger is the most prevalent negative emotion within the three perspectives, so this type of emotion is not only part of stress, but is also an emotion that is attached to the human being.

Stress typology and stress management

According to the Institute of Social Security and Social Services for State Workers (ISSSTE, 2016), there are two classifications of stress: eustress—positive stress—and distress—negative stress. Positive stressors can be: a great joy, professional success, a love date. The person who experiences positive stress is characterized by being creative and motivated. This kind of stress is used as an auxiliary for professional and personal growth. In contrast, distress is anything that produces an unpleasant sensation. It can be an overload of work that the individual cannot assimilate in a simple way, generating a physiological and psychological imbalance. Ordinary life is full of negative stressors, such as failures, family breakdowns, bad work or family environment.

Miller and Smith (1994) recognize the existence of three different types of stress: acute stress, episodic acute stress and chronic stress.

- Acute stress: the most common, easy to manage.
- Episodic acute stress: more severe, suffered by people resistant to change.
- Chronic stress: generated by traumatic circumstances in childhood, leading to violence, suicide, heart attacks and cancer.

The reason for reconsidering the importance of stress management is due to the series of consequences generated by its inadequate control, both physical and psychological. The physical consequences are represented by gastrointestinal, cardiovascular, dermatological or respiratory disorders, while the psychological consequences include

General Techniques	Techniques Cognitive-Behavioral	Relaxation techniques
• Avoid coffee, alcohol and tobacco. Balanced diet. • Doing physical activity, distracting yourself with fun activities.	• Observing oneself and everyday life with a sense of realism. Understanding stressful situations • Assertive, social and control skills training.	• Muscle relaxation • Autogenous relaxation and breath control.

Figure 4.2 Prevention of stress.
Source: Own elaboration based on ISSSTE (https://www.gob.mx/issste).

a lack of control, mental blockages, hypersensitivity to criticism, bad moods and an increase in the probability of suffering accidents and consuming toxic substances (ISSSTE, 2016).

The Institute of Social Security and Social Services for State Workers (ISSSTE, 2016) notes all the consequences that negative stress generates, not only in terms of health but also in the personal context, producing deterioration in interpersonal relationships, within the family, in the workplace and creating high probabilities of breakups. Therefore, this institution has issued some general, cognitive and relaxation techniques in order to prevent stress. In the area of nutrition, it proposes the adoption of less sedentary lifestyles, among others. It favors stress control; self-knowledge continues to be a key point in the regulation of behaviors. Carrying out a daily mental exercise to establish a connection with oneself is a constant that various authors mention. (See Figure 4.2)

For the Regional Institute for Occupational Safety and Health (2011), there are other techniques to manage stress by combating its three levels of response: thoughts, behaviors and physiological activation, with the aim of ending the cycle. The following are described:

- Cognitive system control techniques: carried out when a recurrent thought is detected, it is decided to make a thought stop and carry out a self-instruction, in which constant messages are issued aimed at changing the thought in a positive way.

- Motor system techniques: which are carried out by adopting an assertive communication style, saying the word "no", setting limits, using "I" messages so as not to blame the other person for what you are feeling. The basic steps outlined in this technique are identifying the problem, writing down possible solutions and making decisions.
- Techniques of physiological system control: the establishment of actions that lead to relaxation of the body. Abdominal breathing is one option. The practice of activities such as yoga, Pilates, tai chi, and so on, encourage the release of stress, promoting relaxation.

There are other types of techniques to manage stress, through cognitive, motor and physiological control. It is perceived that the subject has within his or her reach, tools for the regulation of tension, oppression and negative emotions generated by stress. It is a matter of will to choose a lifestyle that is close to peace or not.

Individual optimism

What differentiates optimistic people from those who are not? Beginning with its definition, Blas (2015) indicates that the word "optimism", which originates from the Latin *optimum*, meaning "the best", is conceptualized as the tendency to expect the future to bring favorable results, as well as to perceive the positive aspects of each situation, person or oneself. In this regard, the question arises: why does tolerance to frustration have as an indicator the optimistic disposition to change? Probably this is because it is the ability to always hope for the best in adverse events. It is suggested as a tool of emotional intelligence, since people who possess it tend to build environments free of violence.

What about pessimistic people, are they prone to violent coexistence? To try to answer these questions, it is necessary to go into the definition of the concept, study it, assess it and try to understand more about its nature in order to know if it is possible to acquire this characteristic, or if time, age and experiences are factors that can generate it.

Reviewing the definitions of optimism and pessimism, Blas (2015) points out that they are interpretative tendencies or explanatory styles that people have acquired to explain their individual perception of the reality they experience. This mental representation of external reality depends on their mental model, from which they make an interpretation. Regarding the concept of optimism, in a basic way, the Larousse dictionary (2012) defines it as a propensity to see things from the most favorable perspective. It is perceived that subjects who choose to be optimistic are inclined to predict the best in adverse events. This predisposition is probably the result of an individual and voluntary process. It is the subject's continuous choice to build an environment of well-being, without allowing unexpected situations to modify his or her perception.

For Blas (2015), optimism is a psychological resource that can be learned, in case it has not been developed, because it allows a person to connect with an adequate response to the diverse events of daily life. Any situation, no matter how adverse it may be, can be transformed with creativity, changing a difficulty into an opportunity for growth.

Reflecting on what Blas mentions, it is feasible that anyone can learn to be optimistic. The area of opportunity that needs to be reinforced is people's capacity for creativity. Imagining and creating different alternatives in the face of unfavorable scenarios in everyday life requires training, for which such training is not seen in the education system or in family education, at least in countries like Mexico, where reading to children, an action that favors the imagination, is a rare habit.

For some authors, the optimistic tendency is not synonymous with well-being. Pérez-Álvarez (1992), in his article on positive psychology, identifies seven authors who identify with his idea and are mentioned below. Where optimistic expectations about changes in satisfaction within a marriage depend on the ability of the spouses to confirm them, neither being optimistic nor receiving optimism improves a couple's relationship. According to McNutly and Fincham (cited in Pérez-Álvarez, 1992), positive processes can sometimes be detrimental, while negative behaviors can be beneficial. These authors observe that an understanding of the human condition requires knowledge of psychological traits, which are neither positive nor negative. Their implications depend on the context in which they operate. For their part, Oishi, Diener and Lucas (cited in Pérez-Álvarez, 1992) indicate that too much optimism and happiness can be detrimental. For positive psychology, everything related to happiness, optimism and well-being must be contextualized and nuanced, and Wood and Tarrier (2010) suggest that psychological flexibility may be an important key to well-being.

As Wood and Tarrier (2010) note, the optimistic attitude in everyday life is not so productive in some contexts, for example, when one is in a dynamic of violence. This type of attitude encourages the continuation of a cycle in which there is a positive idea that one day the violent person will change. However, positive psychology does present as a key point that psychological flexibility in people, more than optimism, and the willingness to change perspective and adopt new behaviors in the face of adverse situations that arise in the everyday life, are favorable for well-being. Within couple relationships, it is perceived that, if one of the individuals has this type of flexibility, the existence of negotiation in dialogue as a usual method within the couple dynamic would be probable. Given this dynamic, the question arises, what kind of affection or affection favors peace or tranquility in the couple?

According to Watson and Tellengen (1985, as cited in Díez & Mirón, 2004), in consensus with various authors, affection is manifested in two dimensions, positive and negative. Positive affection represents pleasant emotions, motivation, energy, feelings of mastery and success; people who have a high positive affection usually experience: satisfaction, enthusiasm, friendship, union and confidence. Watson and Tellengen observe that negative affect is related to emotions of discomfort, manifested by fear, frustration, failures and insecurities; it provokes disinterest, boredom, sadness, anguish, shame and envy in people who possess it in greater quantities.

Optimistic readiness for change

Change is defined as a process through which one moves from one state to another, generating quantitative or qualitative modifications to reality. According to León (2002, as cited in López et al., 2013), changes are common in human beings and society, but people do not usually assimilate their repercussions quickly, which is why they produce certain disorders. According to Vera-Villarroel, Valenzuela, Lillo, Martín and Milos (2008, as cited in (Londoño Pérez et al., 2013), this type of trend has been scientifically studied for the last ten years by positive psychology.

People's lack of ability to adapt to a new context is perceived to be generated by mental resistance. The need to have control over what happens in reality can be a factor that clouds inner peace and inhibits harmonious coexistence. If change is a natural process, the best thing would be to educate about it, understanding that, just as the human body changes with age, so do circumstances, people and so forth, so that the individual begins to change his or her thinking and stops opposing and resisting the idea that the future will bring the best.

Returning to the definitions, optimism is a type of intelligence, which is related to self-esteem, as people who tend to have this type of thinking perceive positive aspects of their personality and recognize the capabilities they have and the achievements they have made over time (Blas, 2015). Ji, Zhang, Usborne and Guan (2004, as cited in Londoño et al., 2013) identify dispositional optimism—also referred to as OD—and define it by a regularly stable set of positive expectations about future events. It is a type of coping as opposed to pessimism. OD is perceived as a stable trait throughout life; it tends to reflect emotional stability as time goes by.

In the 1980s, Dan Baker, in his book *What Happy People Know*, pointed out the importance of negative thoughts and the decrease they produce in people's health. In contrast, when positive thoughts are maintained, the mood improves, a state of relaxation prevails and physical discomfort disappears. In conclusion, studies indicate the transforming power of positive thinking in human health (Teruel, 2015). Given the benefits that different authors have suggested regarding positive thoughts, can anyone transform negative thoughts? How can we learn to be optimistic? Given these questions, it is necessary to investigate the learning alternatives proposed by some models.

Skill 3: Tolerance to frustration   149

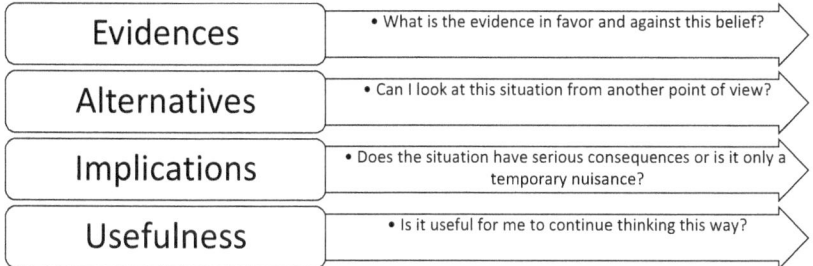

Figure 4.3 Questioning beliefs.
Source: Own elaboration based on Blas (2015).

Taking Blas (2015) as a reference, we describe the ABCDE model of optimistic learning, of which the name means: A: adversity, B: beliefs, C: consequences, D: discussion, E: energization or resolution. This type of analysis makes possible to control and observe people's moods and to change negative emotions by offering positive solutions. As a first step, the ABC is identified, which refers to the problem and the negative emotions it generates; then the pessimistic beliefs are questioned through questions of: evidence, alternatives, implications and usefulness (see Figure 4.3).

At the end of the questioning of beliefs, Blas, the author of the model, notes that it is necessary to obtain a resolution, to conclude the emotions that were generated by the exercise and to generate a more positive transformation of thinking.

The themes of self-analysis, reflection and introspection are constant. Knowledge of the emotional world has to be an indispensable theme in the development of the human being, encouraging silence for the recognition and questioning of belief systems and unconscious patterns that favor repetitive situations, which must be detected from childhood in order to transform them.

For Seligman (2003, as cited in Londoño et al., 2013), optimistic beliefs can be analyzed under the reference of three optics: a) internality/externality: refers to the degree to which a person evaluates himself as responsible for certain events. b) stability/instability: refers to the permanence of the events, whether they will be forever or are transitory. c) globality/specificity: is the degree of generalizing or making an event specific. Referring to the points made by Seligman, a close relationship with the principles of neurolinguistic programming is perceived. The types of techniques discussed in the chapter on assertive language focus the attention on events always with a positive and specific perspective, using every obstacle as an opportunity.

Optimistic intelligence allows us to be aware that any emotion can be managed and controlled. It functions as a compass that is able to orientate how the emotional world is. It has the power to generate situations of: joy, gratitude, serenity, hope, pride, fun, inspiration, interest and love (Blas, 2015). The optimistic disposition to change, as previously reviewed, concerns the tendency that the individual chooses. This tendency will be selected according to the valuation system that his or her mind processes. According to this premise, the issue of the types of mind that exist in the human being is presented.

It would be necessary to locate the type of mindset that a person has in order to have a context that can predict whether or not he or she is able to adopt a positive disposition to change, which is directly related to a high tolerance to frustration and indicates a degree of control over the person's emotions. Riso (2013) describes the three types of mind that people can have: *the rigid mind, the liquid mind and the flexible mind.*

1. People with rigid mindsets or inflexible thinking generate high levels of stress and depression; low FT; anxiety about not being in control; authoritarianism, prejudice, rejection and aggression in interpersonal relationships; difficulty in decision-making; fear of making mistakes and difficulty in personal growth.
2. The liquid mind is empty, apathetic and undefined, fickle and unable to define itself. It does not know itself; therefore, it can remain inconstant, without clear ideas, not making decisions; the person with this type of mentality, as he has no identity, does not commit himself and tends to follow what others say and do.
3. The flexible mind is at the midpoint of the rigid and liquid mentalities, since it has ideas, beliefs and opinions, but is willing to listen to other proposals, and changing its opinion and attitude does not cause problems. The three principles of this type of mind are: the exception to the rule, the middle way and pluralism.

Riso (2013) describes some techniques to create a flexible mind, of which he highlights the practice of empathy in relationships, making it a habit. It is essential to know the ego that every person has, to humbly accept continuous learning and to encourage self-observation as a way of life in order to establish a constant evolution. Among the benefits of a flexible mentality is good judgment, as a person's open mind allows them to make good decisions and establish kind and empathetic relationships with the people they relate to. This type of person manages to live in peace with themselves, easily resolves their problems, and their levels of stress and depression remain low (Riso, 2013).

The recognition of frustrating situations in the course of human life is indispensable. Animals suffer from it and, unlike them, the characteristic reasoning that distinguishes humans from the animal world makes it possible to question situations that produce emotions such as anger. Through constant evaluation, it is possible to find solutions that favor the acceptance of circumstances that cannot be controlled. It is necessary through communication and education programs to disseminate antidotes to stress. Adequate stress management is related to the belief system, self-esteem, nutrition and exercise. It is necessary to return to coexistence with nature, or an adequate administration of time, a factor that is generally distributed in an inadequate way, generating imbalances in marriage, family and work.

A relevant point is the role of the family in strengthening the child's internal control. The formation of personal resources that will allow them to accept situations they do not like in their adult life is a tool that should be nurtured from childhood so that it is easier to deal with the outside world. Fostering a culture of peace involves promoting programs that teach emotional intelligence, the development of positive attitudes, and the promotion of emotional resilience that allows obstacles to be seen as areas of opportunity. Encourage the culture of effort that other generations have used as an anchor to excel and achieve goals.

Reflection questions

1. What is frustration tolerance?
2. What are the four possible sources of violent behavior?

3. Are aggression and violence the same thing? State your answer.
4. Name some sources of frustration
5. What strategies and activities are suggested to promote frustration tolerance?
6. What are the stages of frustration therapy?
7. What is stress?
8. What are some symptoms of stress?
9. What does the Holmes-Rahe scale measure?
10. What do you understand by optimistic readiness to change?

References

Amarista, F. (2008). *La Violencia.* Recuperado el 5 de febrero de 2016, de Gac Méd Caracas: www.scielo.org.ve/scielo.php?pid=S0367-47622008000400002&script=sci_arttext

Blas, V. (2015). *La Inteligencia Optimista.* Buenos Aires: V&R.

Cano Vindel, A., & Miguel Tobal, J. (2001). *Ansiedad y Estrés.* Recuperado el 28 de septiembre de 2014, de Emociones y salud: www.psiquiatria.com/ansiedad/emociones-y-salud/

Chapi Mori, J. L. (marzo de 2012). *Una Revisión Psicologica a las Teorías de Agresividad.* Recuperado el 2 de febrero de 2016, de Revista Electronica de Psicología Iztacala: www.revistas.unam.mx/index.php/repi/article/download/30905/28638

Díez Jorge, M. E., & Mirón Pérez, M. D. (2004). Una paz femenina. En B. Molina Rueda, & F. Muñoz, *Manual de Paz y Conflictos* (págs. 68–93). Granada: Universidad de Granada.

Hurtado, M., De la Cruz, P., & Robles, X. (2015). *Manejo de Frustracón en los niños.* Recuperado el 4 de febrero de 2016, de Instituto Educativo Humanitas: www.se-humanitas.com.mx/autoadministrable/PDF/formacion_padres/07.pdf

INEGI. (noviembre de 2015). *Módulo de Práctica Deportiva y Ejercicio Físico.* Recuperado el 28 de enero de 2016, de INEGI: www.inegi.org.mx/saladeprensa/boletines/2016/especiales/especiales2016_01_08.pdf

Instituto Regional de Seguridad y Salud en el Trabajo. (2011). *Control del Éstres.* Recuperado el 20 de febrero de 2016, de ADEPESCA MADRID: www.adepesca.com/files/documento/manual_de_taller_estres_adepesca_2012.pdf

ISSSTE. (19 de enero de 2016). *Guia para el Estrés, Causas, Consecuencias y Prevención.* Recuperado el 2 de febrero de 2016, de Instituto de Seguridad y Servicios Sociales de los Trabajadores del Estado: www.issste.gob.mx/images/downloads/instituto/prevencion-riesgos-trabajo/Guia-para-el-Estres.pdf

Larousse Diccionario Básico de la Lengua Española. (2012). *Larousse Diccionario Básico de la Lengua Española.* Ciudad de México: Ultra, S.A. de C.V.

Londoño Pérez, C., Hernández Cortés, L. M., Alejo Castañeda, I. E., & Pulido Garzón, D. (enero–marzo de 2013). *Diseño y Valoración de la Escala de*

Optimismo Dispoicional/ Pesimismo-EOP. Recuperado el 9 de febrero de 2016, de Universidad Psychologica: www.redalyc.org/pdf/647/64728729014.pdf

López Dunque, M. E., Restrepo de Ocampo, L. E., & López Velásques, G. L. (abril de 2013). *Resistencia al cambio en organizaciones modernas.* Recuperado el 3 de febrero de 2016, de Scientia Et Technica: www.redalyc.org/articulo.oa?id=8492 7487022

Maroto, M. (2015). *¿Estresado Yo?* Ciudad de México: Pax México .

Menéndez, O. (2008). *Rompiendo Lazos.* Barcelona: Obelisco.

Miller, L., Dell Smith, A., & Rothstein, L. (1994). *Los Distintos tipos de estrés.* Recuperado el 27 de mayo de 2015, de American Psychological Association: www.apa.org/centrodeapoyo/tipos.aspx

Oliva Delgado, A., Antolín Suárez, L., Pertegal Vega, M. Á., Ríos Bermúdez, M., Parra Jiménez, Á., & Hernándo Gómez, Á. (2011). *Instrumentos para evaluar el desarrollo positivo adolescente y los activos familiares, escolares y comunitarios que lo promueven.* Recuperado el 14 de marzo de 2015, de Andalucía Consejería de Salud: http://personal.us.es/oliva/INSTRUMENTOS_DESARROLLO%20P OSITIVO.pdf

OMS. (2004). *La organización del trabajo y el estrés.* Recuperado el 17 de febrero de 2016, de Organización Mundial de la Salud: www.who.int/occupational_health/publications/pwh3sp.pdf

Pérez-Álvarez, M. (2012). La Psicología Positiva: Magia Simpatica. Recuperado el 13 de febrero de 2016, de Papeles del Psicologo: www.papelesdelpsicologo.es/pdf/2137.pdf

Piqueras Rodríguez, J. A., Ramos Linares, V., Martínez González, A. E., & Oblitas Guadalupe, L. A. (diciembre de 2009). *Suma Psicológica.* Recuperado el 23 de septiembre de 2014, de Emociones negativas y su impacto en la salud física y mental: www.redalyc.org/pdf/1342/134213131007.pdf

Real Academia Española. (2016a). *Violenta* . Recuperado el 19 de octubre de 2016, de Diccionario de la Real Academia Española: http://dle.rae.es/?id=brjKWH1

Real Academia Española. (2016b). *Agresivo.* Recuperado el 19 de octubre de 2016, de Diccionario de la Real Academia Española: http://dle.rae.es/?id=19Y31Cf

Redorta, J., Obiols, M., & Bisquerra, R. (2006). *Emoción y Conflicto.* Barcelona: Paidós Ibérica.

Riso, W. (2013). *El Poder del Pensamiento Flexible.* Ciudad de México: Océano.

Ruetti, E., & Justel, N. (2010). *Bases Neurobiológicas de la Frustración.* Recuperado el 2 de febrero de 2016, de Revista Argentina de Ciencias del Comportamiento: www.redalyc.org/articulo.oa?id=333427070006

Santiago Lopezó, S. (2001). *Programa de Intervención para mejorar la estabilidad emocional.* Recuperado el 5 de febrero de 2016, de Clínica y Salud: www.redalyc.org/pdf/1806/180618319005.pdf

Teruel, A. (2015). *Inteligencia Emocional Para Todos.* Ciudad de México: Lectorum.

Torres, X., & Baillés, E. (2014). *Comprender el estrés.* Barcelona: Amat.

Wood, A. M., & Tarrier, N. (2010). Positive clinical psychology. A new vision and strategy for integrated research and practice. *Clinical Psychology Review*, 30, 819–829.

Chapter 5

Culture of peace with an approach to the gender perspective in marriage

Nature of the culture of peace

In order to understand the nature of the culture of peace, it is necessary to understand some basic questions to explore its meaning, questions such as: What is peace and the culture of peace? What are its origins? Who are or who were the people who initiated it and who currently promote it? This section aims to answer these questions.

What is peace? is a question that has been asked by researchers since the postwar period of the 1950s. Although authors such as Fisas (1978, as cited in Coca et al., 2015) situate peace studies as beginning in the 1930s with Sorokin's research in the Department of Sociology at Harvard University, other authors note that it was in the 1940s when peace studies was born with the aim of preventing wars. After World War II, followed by the Cold War, the concern changed, and by the 1950s the objective was the elimination of nuclear weapons, giving rise to other lines of analysis (Martínez et al., 1995). The concept of peace appears over time linked to the concept of war. Muñoz (1993, as cited in Muñoz & López, 2000) points out that although the nonexistence of peace can be affirmed without the presence of war, the yearning of people for peace in the face of war generated its origin. At that stage, due to the lack of analysis of the concept, it received the name "peace ideology". With the development of the concept of peace, as Muñoz points out, it was associated with other fields related to altruism, cooperation, love, solidarity and so on. In the last stage of the development of the concept following the World Wars, the construction of peace theory emerged, and finally, from a scientific perspective and due to advances in the social sciences, peace research came about.

Approaching a conceptual definition of peace, Jiménez (2009) indicates that peace comes from the Greek word *Eirene*, defined as the absence of war or a pause between two conflicts. *Eirene* for the Greeks is the synonym of harmony, a concept related to a state of calm, tranquility, a mental, exterior, soulful harmony and that is attributed to peaceful feelings. After the Romans conquered the Greeks, the concept of peace was termed *pax*. For the Romans the term was used to name agreements between people or groups. Its definition according to Lederach (2000, as cited in Cabello, 2012) was related to respecting what is legal within interpersonal relationships, as a way of maintaining order.

Over the course of time, and as will be discussed later in this chapter, the concept of peace developed not only as the absence of war, as the Greco-Roman culture had pointed out, but went beyond a state of serenity and harmony. This new definition would involve issues related to equality, equity, development, social justice and culture.

Taking up the concept again, another definition of peace states that it is a symptom of well-being, prosperity, calm. It provides union with others, nature and the universe; peace provides humanity. It gives meaning to life in order to relate to others and find pleasant solutions to conflicts. It is an antidote to selfishness and any form of violence (Muñoz, 2004). For Johan Galtung (1996, as cited in Jiménez, 2009), peace is defined as the willingness to address conflict with empathy, nonviolence and creativity. This concept has been studied in different areas of the social sciences, such as politics and sociology, in the area of history, and from the approaches of nonviolence, conflict, reconciliation, security, disarmament and victimology (Coca et al., 2015).

As seen in the ideology of Coca et al., peace is described as a state of tranquility, a symptom of well-being and a readiness to approach conflict with empathy. The reconstruction of peace is perceived as a state of mind, which results in feelings of calm and creates the necessary conditions for peaceful conflict resolution.

Another concept worth mentioning is that of coexistence. Authors such as Maturana (1984, as cited in Ministry of Women and Social

Development, 2009) indicate that coexistence means living with each other, based on subjective value codes that are found within a given social context. Coexistence is associated with conflict, but this does not mean that threat, conflict and coexistence are realities of the way of living in society. Within marriage, the phenomenon of human coexistence is a factor that generates conflict, which can be considered part of human nature.

This type of coexistence is intended to be peaceful, so it is proposed to resolve conflicts through active listening, assertive language and tolerance toward frustration, purposes aligned with the objectives of the culture of peace. Combining the concepts of coexistence, peace and marriage represents a great effort in which different sectors are involved. At a cultural level, it signifies a challenge due to the naturalization of violent coexistence that begins in courtship and continues in marriage, leading to a cycle of violence for generations that is learned and replicated by the children.

For Galtung (1981, as cited in Martinez et al., 1995), the principle of peace research is to seek to reduce violence, whether direct or structural. The nature of peace research seeks to understand conflict in order to identify processes, policies and mechanisms to reduce the rates of it. Initially, the value of peace research was non-war, but later the value of justice was incorporated, economically and socially. The same authors point out that at present, peace research encompasses a broad agenda of work, involving the origins, evolution and prevention of conflicts in relation to issues of economic inequality, human rights, environmental crisis, poverty, ethnic and religious issues, among others.

Concept and evolution of the culture of peace

In pointing out the concept and evolution of the culture of peace, it is necessary to mention the two definitions—of culture and of peace—separately. Culture has a very broad meaning as well as does peace, which was discussed in the previous section. In this section, the aim is to investigate the definition of culture and to try to understand more about the origin of the culture of peace and its transformation over time.

For H. Goodenough (1975, as cited in Jiménez, 2009), the culture of a society is everything it believes and knows, with the purpose of acting in a way that is acceptable to the members to which it belongs. Culture is a set of historical and social constructions that have allowed the human race to survive, so they are not eternal and their continuity depends on the ability to enable and facilitate life. Culture is not a monolithic unit, but is formed by a set of atavistic imaginaries and meanings that give meaning to human actions (Martínez, 2015). The same author defines atavistic imaginaries as those unquestionable learnings that define the logic of human relationships and nature, are transmitted from past times from generation to generation, and can be followed consciously or unconsciously, forming the backbone of culture.

The concept of the culture of peace, historically was a term proposed by the priest Felipe Mac Gregor, who headed the National Standing Commission for Peace Education in Peru. In 1986, Mac Gregor, with a team of people, had published the book *Culture of Peace in Peru*, in which the author had already developed definitions of conflict, violence and peace. For Félix Martí, the culture of peace is the opposite of the ancestral philosophy of an eye for an eye; he defines it as a social movement, with cultural, political and academic aims to change the culture of the world (Ministerio de la Mujer y Desarrollo Social, 2009).

Continuing with the concept of the culture of peace, it has remained through time and continues its evolution. It had to be supported in various events and movements that have collaborated and have contributed strength to the subject, among them, peace movements, which are described below. The pacifist movements have been relevant to dismantling the legitimacy of violence, defined by López (2004) from a negative perspective as the social response to war, and from a positive perspective as a doctrine that seeks to favor a state of peace between people, states and peoples. Martínez (2015) describes some social movements:

- Reflections for peace have made visible the real reasons for war and the economic interests that lie behind false freedom struggles.

- The feminist revolution has served to teach us about the construction of gender violence, which arises from generation to generation, and how to deconstruct it.
- The environmental movement has taken an interest in the destruction of the ecosystem to deconstruct violence against nature.
- The hippie movement in the 1960s changed the perception of war.
- Some Vietnam War veterans became pacifists.
- In 2003, demonstrations took place against the war in Iraq. The first global mobilization was carried out through virtual media.
- The Arab springs where Arab society was manifested by the oppression of the rulers. Action that promoted non-violence.
- The nonviolent 15M movement in Spain had as a principle not to flee a conflict, without attending to violent actions such as aggression, intimidation, threats or confrontations.

Another relevant document that served as a flag to combat violence, was the Seville Manifesto of 1986 ((Ministerio de la Mujer y Desarrollo Social, 2009; Ministry of Women and Social Development). Prepared by a group of scientists, it was disseminated by UNESCO and described the following:

- Scientifically, it is incorrect to mention that a tendency to make war has been inherited from ancestors.
- It is wrong to suggest that violent behavior is pre-established in human genetics.
- It is wrong to say that the human being has a brain of a violent type, since there is nothing that forces a person to choose violent behavior.
- Human biology does not condemn war. It is the human species that has invented war; therefore, it is the responsibility of each individual to create peace.

The manifesto reflects the position of science regarding the genetic predisposition of the human being to engage in violent behaviors.

The imbalance of power and evidence of the lack of a coexistence free of violence are social constructions created by man and imitated by generations. In no case is someone born with a violent tendency.

The repeated actions that have generated atavistic imaginaries continue to be valid due to a lack of introspection on the part of the individual, an activity that generates questions about behaviors that have been passed down from generation to generation. No reference is made to the fact that the entire culture of Mexico is negative; on the contrary, it represents a great richness that distinguishes the country on a global level. The key point where our attention is focused is on affective relationships, especially within marriage, where there are relevant deficiencies that have not been identified and worked on specifically to improve the quality of coexistence, as atavistic imaginaries continue to prevail that do not allow relationships based on equality and that favor the care of both spouses, causing power to be unbalanced and giving rise to violence. This type of repetitive behavior does not occur in all marriages. It would be wrong to overgeneralize. According to statistics, there is a population that is not involved in violent behavior, and that is precisely the object of this research study: to discover these components that have developed in couples who may not have followed these negative atavistic imaginaries.

Social movements contribute to the birth of a new culture as a condition of survival. Eric Tello (n.d., as cited in Martínez, 2015) talks about the new culture of participation with conscience, which breaks with hierarchical structures at all levels. Conscience, a component proposed by Tello, turns out to be the central axis of this type of social movement that has originated nowadays. People who participate in these movements feel a genuine intention to improve the quality of life of humanity, where new forms of coexistence are chosen, and there is an openness toward tolerance and respect for differences.

For Vincent Martínez Guzmán (2002, as cited in Reid et al., 2002) it is a relevant social transformation of a global nature initiated by humanity. Another source of the concept of culture of peace is that it was born after World War II, in which more than 100 million people lost their lives. In 1945 the UN was created, with the aim of protecting future generations from war, and in that same year UNESCO was created, with the objective of promoting cooperation in education, science and culture to fulfill the purposes of peace (Ministry of Women and Social Development, 2009).

When addressing the issue of peace as a concept of culture of peace, Sanchez (2010) points out that it is indicative of a continuous process of construction, is dynamic in nature, and therefore not confined to a particular period of time. Sanchez points out that the culture of peace is in a continuous process of construction. Previously, the challenge implied by the union of two concepts: culture and peace, both with disproportionate definitions, was pointed out. Therefore, introducing it into daily coexistence requires constant work, where the individual, before practicing peaceful interaction with their surroundings, needs to be educated to calm their mind, thoughts and exercise an identification of emotions to control their behavior.

Returning to the historical line of the culture of peace concept, it was not until 1989, when the international congress called Peace in the Minds of Men was held in Yamoussoukro (Ivory Coast), that the concept of the culture of peace was used for the first time. The congress invited participants to build a new culture of peace based on respect for life, tolerance for human rights and equality between men and women (Ministry of Women and Social Development, 2009). It was at this moment in history when, through the congress, conflict related to the imbalance of power between men and women became evident, in which the focus is placed on affective relationships. It is recognized that looking at women only as victims will not solve the problem; rather, the perspective of the analysis had to be comprehensive, looking at the problem as a bilateral, family, transgenerational and cultural issue.

The culture of peace, according to the first article of the Declaration of the United Nations Action Program on a Culture of Peace, is a set of values, attitudes, traditions and behaviors that are based on respect for life, and the elimination of violence through the practice of the philosophy of nonviolence, dialogue, education and cooperation (Cabello, 2012).

Culture of peace 161

> Accepting the other: this involves recognizing their peace, their truth and their error.

> Respect for human dignity: we are all equal.

> Addressing differences in a construtive way: focusing on solutions, analyzing unspoken fears and listening to each other in an empathic way.

> Activating cooperative processes: engagement

Figure 5.1 Keys to making peace.
Source: Own elaboration based on Martínez (2022, as cited in Reid et al., 2002).

Martinez (2002, as cited in Reid et al., 2002) prefers to call the culture of peace proposed by UNESCO a culture of "peacemaking". Peacemaking is an action on both sides; the indicator of peacemaking favors attention and allows for a more sensitive disposition to the ways in which different cultures live in peace.

As can be seen in Figure 5.1, the starting point is to accept the other with their mistakes and virtues, to respect equality, to solve differences constructively through empathy, and finally to establish a commitment to the agreement that has been established. The methodology used by Martinez for making peace is interesting and its results would activate cooperative processes. What is observed is that steps continue to be taken to relate to others, when in order to generate a process of acceptance toward others, it is necessary to create acceptance toward oneself, which requires time, training and internalization, as well as processes that strengthen the individual's self-esteem.

Table 5.1 Evolution of the concept of a culture of peace

1992	UNESCO establishes programs to promote the culture of peace in Central America and Africa.
1994	The first forum on the Culture of Peace is held in El Salvador.
1995	UNESCO in its 28th conference establishes the concept of culture of peace in its 1996–2001 strategy.
1996–2001	UNESCO establishes the project: Towards a Culture of Peace.
1997	The United Nations declares 2000 as the International Year for the Culture of Peace.
1998	The UN declares the period 2001–2010 as the International Decade for a Culture of Peace and Non-Violence for the Children of the World.
1999	The UN declares the Program of Action on the Culture of Peace
2000	The 2000 Manifesto Campaign is implemented.

Source: Ministry of Woman and Social Development (2009).

For Boulding (1996, as cited in Cabello, 2012), the culture of peace introduces a lifestyle, values and behaviors, attitudes that contribute to the well-being, equality, security of individuals, groups and nations, without using violence. Such actions benefit the construction of a culture of peace. Dialogue is the way to solve conflict. It is the way in which dynamics of encounter are generated to reach peace; therefore, there must be a culture of dialogue: it is about listening well to what the other has to say to find the point of rapprochement. If there is no dialogue, there is no democracy either; thus, there will always be human rights problems (Reid et al., 2002). (See Table 5.1)

Article 3 of the Declaration and Program of Action on a Culture of Peace (1999) states that the development of a culture of peace is linked to the possibility for all people to obtain tools for dialogue, negotiation, consensus and peaceful dispute resolution (Ministry of Women and Social Development, 2009). The relevance of producing a book such as this one is aligned with the culture of peace action program. The study that was carried out shows small actions that integrate dialogue, which can obstruct, block and complicate the development of verbal violence.

The typology of peace in the twenty-first century

The typology of peace in the twenty-first century is the union of different models of peace that have been proposed over time. The aim is to describe the definitions of each type of peace, in order to generate a comprehensive understanding of the proposals that peace research authors have suggested for the elimination of different types of violence. Before approaching the typology of peace, it is necessary to investigate the categorization of violence.

Galtung (2003, as cited in Calderón, 2009) identifies three dimensions of violence: direct violence, structural violence and cultural violence, which are described below:

- Direct violence: manifests itself physically, verbally or psychologically.
- Structural violence: this is violence for which social, political and economic systems are responsible, because they generate poverty, inequality and social injustice within the population.
- Cultural violence: is the result of inherited traditions, ideology, religion and ancestral behaviors that legitimize violence.

In situating the problem, the emotional violence that occurs in Mexican couples can be seen as direct violence, which is the result of a cultural violence in which the patriarchal system, learned from generation to generation, places the man in a superior position of power. Moreover, it is also perceived that, due to a lack of education generated by structural violence, which causes a lack of basic needs, the population does not have access to adequate education that would allow them to learn to use communication and components of emotional intelligence to regulate their emotions and resolve couple conflicts in a peaceful way.

Different types of peace emerge as a response to violence. One of the researchers who has produced the most studies on peace is the Norwegian Johan Galtung, who has contributed the notions of positive peace, negative peace and cultural peace. Other more recent authors such as Francisco A. Muñoz have added imperfect peace, and the researcher Francisco Jiménez proposed neutral peace.

Looking back in history, in the first stage of scientific studies there were three ways in which the concept of peace was approached: negative peace, referring to the nonexistence of direct and indirect violence; positive peace, in which social justice prevails; and recently neutral peace, which has as its indicator the absence of cultural or symbolic violence (Jiménez, 2009). In the following, each of these ideas of peace is briefly presented.

Muñoz (2004) points out that positive peace is that which is aimed at social justice; negative peace is experienced when there is no war or violence; and imperfect peace is the causal correspondence between peace agencies. Taking Jiménez (2009) as a reference, the following is a description of negative peace, positive peace and neutral peace from Jiménez's perspective:

Negative peace is defined as the absence of armed conflict, which is the result of a dynamic balance of economic, political, cultural and technological factors. The concept was inherited from the Romans, and remained in force until 1959, when Galtung pointed out that negative peace should also include the absence of mistreatment, rape, murder, child abuse and street deaths. Positive peace and structural violence were introduced by Galtung in 1960. He refers to structural violence by pointing out that, as long as there is injustice and a lack of basic human needs, there will be no peace, even if it is not directly visible. Therefore, positive peace is about working for social justice and development so that every human being can meet his or her basic needs.

Neutral peace is peace that is situated in the face of cultural violence, aims to use dialogue as a method and is part of a gradual process. In order to achieve this type of peace, it is necessary to understand the culture of the other through empathy, to acquire tolerance and to appreciate differences as beneficial. The process of neutral peace requires the neutralization of mental schemas, which demands profound alterations that can only be achieved through social and cultural transformation. In this sense, the neutrality of language is fundamental; it is essential that when one person hears a word, he or she has the same value for the other.

Muñoz and Jiménez (2015) have added the concept of imperfect peace, using the adjective imperfection to situate peace semantically as unfinished, in the process of construction, with the probability of the development in human relations and coexistence in which peace predominates over violence. According to Muñoz and Jiménez, the concept is based on an understanding of the complexity of human, social and environmental relations. However, it is structured by the imperfection of the human being, which makes it possible to continuously learn from mistakes, reconcile oneself and accept the existence of failures and successes in the course of life. Imperfect peace is born within the framework of a transition in which democracy was installed, condemning the civil war and the dictatorship of Francisco Franco in Spain. For Muñoz (2001, as cited in (Jiménez & Muñoz, 2012), peace must be studied based on the different forms, capacities and competences to make peace and not based on violence.

Having pointed out the concept of the culture of peace previously, another peace proposal is the intercultural one, which is directed toward generating cultural dialogue, is built by a planetary civil society, establishes a global peace that is built by all and for all without any type of exclusion, and understands peace as a plural and cultural experience in which one's own experience is not privileged over others (López, 2004).

The typology of peace in the twenty-first century, as based on Jiménez (2009), is summarized in Figure 5.2, starting with negative peace, which occurs in the absence of direct violence. Positive peace is the response to structural violence, which proposes actions aimed at eradicating poverty, inequality and social injustice. Imperfect peace is another alternative aimed at eradicating structural violence through a series of actions that require time. Finally, cultural peace and neutral peace, whose purpose is to promote dialogue to establish empathy, tolerance and to be able to carry out actions that eliminate cultural violence, are closely related to each other because of the purpose that unites them, although each has a different ideology.

Peace is seen as an aspiration and a human need, which can be achieved through the elimination or reduction of direct, structural and cultural violence. Taking as a reference Jiménez (2009), the future second-generation peace—social, *gaia* and internal—and the third-generation peace—multi-/inter-/transcultural—are described.

166 Culture of peace

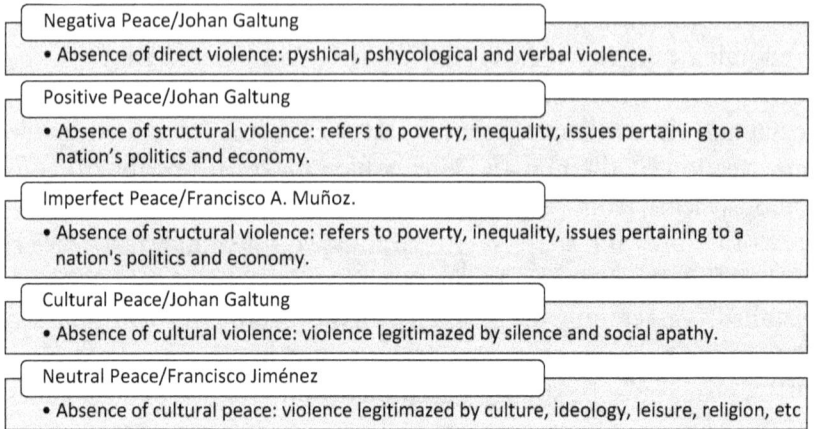

Figure 5.2 Types of peace in the twenty-first century.
Source: Own elaboration based on Jiménez (2009).

Second-generation peace:

- Social peace: is a type of peace that involves all challenges related to all forms of violence, development, democracy, human rights and the environment.
- Gaia peace: refers to ecology or natural peace. The ideology is to do no harm to any living thing on Earth or to the planet.
- Inner Peace: refers to the peace that is found within oneself, that which can only be achieved through introspection. The way to change the world is through inner movements; according to Krishamurti (1973, cited in Jimenez, 2009), the outer is only a reflection of the inner.

Third-generation peace:

Multi-/inter-/transcultural peace, the prefix "multi-/inter" refers to the understanding of peace from a multicultural and intercultural context. It is the idea that the world and societies are made up of individual people, their ideas and thoughts, and that is where culture comes from, so there is no separation. Continuing with the breakdown of the second term, transculturality is intended to enable the individual to extend beyond their cultural framework, to overcome the limitations that their traditions have established and to create more evolved thinking about the conception of peace. Education in critical thinking for the development of competencies, skills and cognitive abilities is the goal of this peace perspective, as big changes are brought about through social transformations. Therefore, building a new multi-/inter-/and transcultural peace requires conscious and responsible human beings. Taking Jiménez Bautista (2011) as a reference, the competences that should be taught to the new generations are the following:

- Instruct in attitudes, rather than change them; the first thing to do is to prevent before curing.
- Try to connect with people from other cultures, to achieve enrichment in others' differences.
- Understand that there are no superior or inferior culture, so do not label one culture as better or worse than another.
- Recognize that each culture is made up of positive and negative aspects, which is why it is necessary to study and value them without opting for ethnocentric views.
- Acknowledge that cultural contributions should be understood in a respectful but also critical way.
- Understand that differences enrich. Take advantage of the great opportunity of learning that each person offers us to strengthen human formation.

The third generation addresses ethnocentrism as a form of violence that eliminates any action for peace. According to Galtung, violence is made up of three types of violence that he describes in a triangle. Jimenez alludes to the fact that it must be approached from all angles, approaches and so on. It is inferred that it must be confronted from all its vertices in order to achieve new peace such as multi-/inter-/and transcultural peace (Jiménez Bautista, 2011). The document that was consulted does not typify imperfect peace and cultural peace, which have been replaced by neutral peace. Jiménez (2009), who carried out the classification, engaged in a debate on imperfect peace and does not consider it to be a type of peace; however, in the table where the generations of peace are summarized, they have been added with the aim of presenting all the types of peace that have been studied. The first, second, third and fourth generations of peace have been graded.

Scientists from Colombia and Spain are researching the fourth-generation peace, such as: sustainable peace, vulnerable peace and resilient peace. The fourth generation, in the same way as the third generation, is focused on the right to peace (Jiménez, 2016). In particular, it reviews the issues that the twenty-first century has brought with it: militarism, nuclear weapons, global conflict, cooperation, human rights, sexism, ethnic conflicts, nuclear development and so on. It also addresses issues of: postmodernity, multidisciplinarity, globalization, conflict acceptance and transformation, participation, empowerment, science and technology for peace, civil society and peace, visions of probable and desired futures, culture of peace and the human right to peace. (Jiménez, 2011).

Although this new generation of peace has not been scientifically and academically recognized, it can be concluded that sustainable, vulnerable and resilient forms of peace are within an emerging generation, which are directly related to the issue of bioethics (Figure 5.3).

An attempt has been made to summarize the typologies of peace in the twenty-first century in a simple way, recognizing the complexity that would be generated by addressing them in depth, as it would require much more than one paper or section to describe the elements, principles and foundations of each one of them. In view of this situation, after reviewing the essence of each of the types of peace, it was concluded that there was a lack of order according to the relevance that each of the paces represents. In this sense, internal peace is perceived as the basis for achieving any other type of peace defined in the generational stages. Educating the new generations in mental control, reflection and self-knowledge, with the aim of recognizing their emotional body and transforming emotions of anger, fear or pain, could be a real antidote to achieving a state of peace that is reflected in interpersonal relationships.

Culture of peace 169

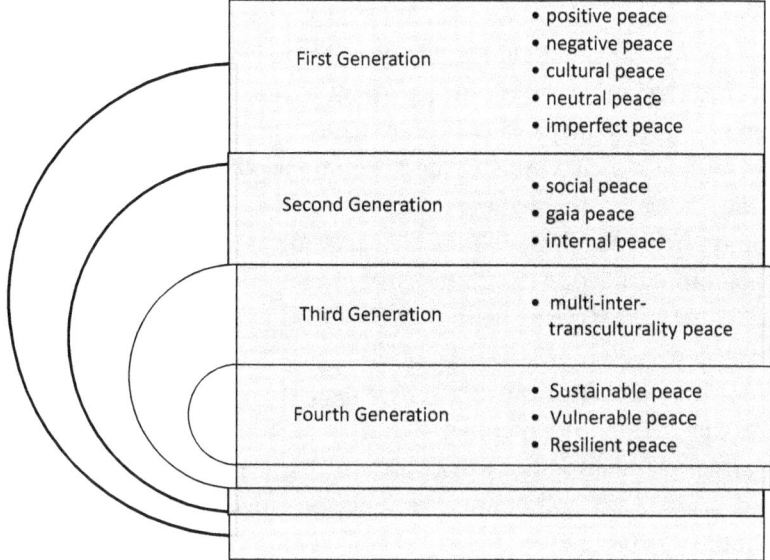

Figure 5.3 Generations of peace.
Source: Own elaboration based on Jiménez (2009).

After investigating the subject of the culture of peace, it is necessary to consider the partners in heterosexual marriage, and the way in which peace has been approached from the male and female perspective as the object of study, a perspective that throughout history has defined different customs for each role, as nowadays other alternatives are proposed that reconstruct practices of equality.

Gender and the culture of peace

The purpose of considering the culture of peace and gender research is to reflect on previous studies that have been carried out since its beginnings, to know its precursors, to present the new masculinities, to observe women as agents of peace and to examine the proposals that the research is creating, with the aim of promoting the reconstruction of gender concepts for the reduction of violence. A position is expressed in which men and women are studied with their biological and natural differences, but with gender equality. This is not a work with feminist or macho overtones. On the contrary, it seeks to find a balance based on equality in order to generate proposals, with the sole purpose of establishing components that favor a culture of peace within marriage.

Gender is a concept that began to be used in the 1970s. Its definition is related to the social and cultural construction of the feminine and masculine, which also has as its objective the study of the conflicting power relations of men, women and society (Díez & Mirón, 2004). Regarding the beginnings of gender studies, it is recorded that it was in the period between 1986 and 1987 when Reardon and Birgit Brock-Utne established an area of research on the gender perspective within peace research. They were in charge of finishing the work started by Elise Boulding, who carried out an analysis of gender violence against women and children (Jiménez, 2009).

But what is a gender perspective? To answer this question, Díez & Sánchez (2010) indicate that it is a new approach that allows the introduction of concepts, hierarchies and interpretations that make it easier to observe the position of women within society, its purpose is to favor the reconstruction of a new configuration, eliminating the patriarchal configuration that has remained for a long time. The concept of a gender perspective is perceived to be unclear and can be understood as a feminist ideology, with the purpose of equalizing women's rights and favoring the subjugation of men. Therefore, it is considered relevant to explain its definition in a simple way, so that the message can be easily understood by people.

It is necessary to identify the basic definitions of terms such as sex and gender, which are two different concepts. The first refers to morphological and functional differences at birth, while the second concept, according to Murillo de la Vega (2001, as cited in (Muñoz & Jiménez, 2010) refers to what is expected of them in life. To understand these notions in a simple way, when we talk about gender, we seek to give women the power that has not been given to them over time, so that they are positioned on an equal footing with men. Gender refers to the fact that both genders are capable of carrying out the same tasks and that, above all, both have the same capacity to express attention, care and affection to their family members.

The role that has been assigned to women throughout history is a role of being in favor of peace, of women with children asking men to go to war, of arguing for the protective masculinity of men and the vulnerable femininity of women, of roles that involve women in peace, when in matters of peace, its construction actually depends on everyone (Díez & Mirón, 2004). It is precisely this role of peace that has been assigned to women over time, which is also intended to make them equal with men. It is a matter of both sexes, more than a gender construction that is intended to be included in the new masculinities; it is a matter of assuming human nature, which is free of competition, power and violence.

Throughout history, essentially in the sixteenth century, men and women were the subject of various discourses aimed at molding their conduct and their role within society. This shaping of their conduct and roles was intended to direct life and perfect behavior; it was the ideal way to follow. It was this outlook in legislation, religion, morality, philosophy, medicine and press that would give rise to the patriarchal prototype, which implanted inequality between men and women (Lado, 2002). The same author points out that later, in the eighteenth century, a discourse would broaden the way in which women should be educated, especially during different stages of their lives. After their first menstruation, they were educated with the sole purpose of being mothers, for whom a good marriage should be ensured, and during adulthood their time should be dedicated to motherhood and the home, it would be until old age when they would receive the appreciation of their family and recognition from society.

In view of yesteryear, questions arise such as: What is the true feminine and masculine nature? Why do we continue with the prototype of centuries ago? Should a concept of feminine or masculine be constructed, or is it the responsibility of each individual to do so? Is society ready, or is there a lack of awareness to construct an individual model? Does gender really have to exist?

The lack of a gender perspective within the categories of analysis, according to Martinez (2010), has corrupted the human species, as men and as women. Due to some research on the female gender, it has been discovered that, with sexism as a system of male domination, women and men have forgotten the human quality. It is the misconceptions of belief systems that increase this problem. There is no superiority of men over women, which is probably the root of the power conflict that is lodged in the being, which has generated confusion in children educated by mothers and fathers who have followed generational patterns without stopping to question about human equality. No one is less or more, which is the true equality that is shared for the simple reason of being human.

In order to promote a culture of peace from a gender perspective, taking Diez and Sánchez (2010) as a reference, the following aspects that need to be implemented are pointed out:

- Within a gender perspective analysis, it is relevant to know the different needs of men and women, and the roles that have been established throughout history and culture, reflecting on the conflicts that have arisen.
- Gender equality should be incorporated into all programs, for both women and men.
- It is important to introduce women and women's organizations into activities aimed at building peace and resolving conflicts with men.
- Incorporating women into decision-making helps ensure that they are included in activities.

Nowadays, more and more women are showing their skills in the media, demonstrating their intellectual capacity and their ability to excel in different academic, social, artistic, sporting and scientific fields, among others. Undoubtedly, there is much to be done so that in the future, the decision for a woman to dedicate herself to home-making will be a free choice based on affective reasons and not on a belief in duty or on a lack of cognitive capacity.

For Comins (2015), research on gender peace has two ways of working: the critical perspective, corresponding to the analysis, diagnosis, denunciation and visibility of violence against women; and the constructive perspective, which refers to focusing attention on women as agents of peace building. It is from the constructivist perspective, as Comins points out, that the focus on women as agents of peace and new masculinities is addressed, where the aim is to use the feminine gender role designated to women as a philosophy of peace that both genders use.

New masculinities

The introduction of the gender perspective as a new vision of reconstructing the concept of masculinity, aimed at the elimination of patriarchy within society, leads to diverse opinions on the subject: mainly from inflexible thinking that resists making changes where the adoption of behaviors and roles that could be considered exclusive to women is accepted.

It is therefore necessary to address what research has shown about masculinities in the twenty-first century. Perhaps for other countries, these types of issues are not relevant because their degree of evolution has been rapid, but in countries like Mexico, where 73.6 percent of men are heads of household (INEGI, 2014), it is an issue that is perceived to be a gradual process toward acceptance and practice. Mainly using terms such as head of household does not favor the construction of peace. If what is intended is that women and men are considered equals, why continue to use terms that classify and point out differences in power within a household? When a marriage is formed by members of a team, in which each one performs different activities that are decided by democratic choice, why is there a need to always highlight someone as superior?

"Head of household" is defined by López (2001, as cited in INEGI, 2014) as the recognition of the most important person by the members of the family, as the one who is always at home, with the greatest authority and who provides the economic support. This is an example of a complicated belief that remains today, which continues to incite and encourage power games within marriage, generating fights between its members and distancing the couple, when what actually is sought in the union of marriage is to encourage rapprochement, dialogue and agreements.

Muñoz (2001, as cited in Jiménez & Muñoz, 2012) points out that the category of gender is necessary in the culture of peace, in order to reconfigure the feminine and the masculine way of being, where there is more flexibility and less violence, from the moral perspective of the ethics of care and the ethics of justice. Facio and Fries (2005, as cited in Gallego, 2015) indicate that through education and the culture of peace, it is necessary to break down traditional stereotypes about the idea that the masculine is the model for humans, for which it is essential to rewrite the roles and concepts of the human being and reinforce a system where equality prevails.

A patriarchal society, as identified approximately 5,000 years ago, is one that transforms the differences in resources in favor of the male sex. From a gender perspective, society is under the dominance of men, although there is influence from women (Muñoz & Jiménez, 2010). Beatty Reardon (1985, as cited in Martínez, 2010) indicates that sexism as male domination arises when men realize from birth the dependence they have on women, who are revealed in a fragile being. Realizing this fragility toward life, produces fear and defensiveness as a form of protection, and then violence is exercised in order to dominate.

For Giner (2010, as cited in Gallego, 2015), boys and girls begin to form their personalities according to the values and images they observe in their families, as they are the primary agents of socialization. It is there where behavior is transmitted and where they learn to recognize a specific social structure. From a historical perspective, there are 5,000 years of patriarchal beliefs. Changing these dogmas requires a gradual but constant process, above all in the area of education and the strengthening of self-esteem. If the root of male domination relies, as Giner and Gallego suggest, on fear, this is produced by insecurities, which is why it is necessary to provide and educate men with more security, to work on their thinking to develop high self-esteem that does not suggest that they opt for subjugation toward women as a way of reinforcing their power.

Male chauvinist gender stereotypes prevail when violence against women is naturalized. This type of behavior is based on a relationship of dominance in which women are considered as inferior or invisible persons. The physical strength of the male sex has been confused with the concept of power, which has led to the erroneous idea that certain prestigious activities are exclusive to men (Gallego Noche, 2015). According to Tobeña Pallarés (1998, as cited in

(Muñoz & Jiménez, 2010), the factor of women's physical fragility has been used as an advantage to position men in a higher place in the social hierarchy.

Gender-based violence is one of the most pressing problems, as it has an impact on social, cultural, health and economic issues, which require multidimensional strategies in their intervention. The probable causes of gender-based violence are: culture, social structures, social crises, and a deficit in communication skills and conflict resolution, among others. The concepts of masculinity and violence, which are often associated, have generated the social image of the violent male as something natural supported by confirmatory objectives, such as "boys are more attracted to violent games than girls" (Hernández Castillo, 2017).

Confusion related to men's physical characteristics are other causes of competition between the sexes. It is a perceived point that needs to be addressed within the culture of peace, the desire for competition. Equal relationships cannot be established if competition is encouraged and others are seen as rivals. It is perceived as a conflict at a cultural level. It is necessary to understand that there is no need to evaluate others to show who is the best. There are no better or worse individuals; rather, there are unique beings, with different intelligences and abilities, each with strengths and weaknesses, with the sole purpose of engaging in constant work to improve the quality of being human.

The configuration of the identity of men and women depends on the way in which relationships are maintained, on the way in which the ties that unite human beings with nature are repaired. There is no way of knowing what is natural if there are no actions of care (Martínez, 2010). The power of the models through which the family teaches literacy is relevant. In the area of equality in education, two models that must be reinforced for gender equality are fundamental: the first is related to violence against women, the second to the role of women in the home (Gallego, 2015).

On the concept of masculinity, Gilmore (1994, as cited in (Fernández, 2010) defines it as an accepted way of being an adult male in a society; Hernández Castillo (2017) mentions that masculinity is understood as ideas or roles typical of the male gender, built by culture, epoch, history, that is, society; Ortega Hegg (2005, as cited in García & Mendizábal, 2015) indicates that masculinity communicates the conviction that men develop as belonging to the male sex, so it is a sociocultural construction, happening in specific conditions of space and time. The proposal for a new masculinity is the acceptance of being fragile and understanding the need to interact with others and with nature. For Boltanski in 2000; Martínez in 2003; Ricoeur in 2005 indicated that new policies are required to confront fears and fragility, to potentiate the skills and competencies that allow for relationships where peace prevails, and where human beings structure their personal identity (Martínez, 2010). For Flecha (2016), there are currently three types of masculinities, as described below:

- Traditional dominant masculinity: refers to the authoritarian model of possession, jealousy and naturalized violence that subjugates the female sex.
- Traditional oppressed masculinity: refers to receiving humiliation from the female sex, submission to domestic chores and inequality.
- New alternative masculinities: is the union between oppressed women and oppressed men. It is based on the creation of a new type of masculinity based on male security and the acceptance of equality between men and women.

Regarding Flecha's classification of masculinities, it would be interesting to carry out research to detect the masculinity that prevails in Mexico today. Perhaps new types of masculinities could be emerging that are different from the traditional dominant masculinities that have long prevailed in the country.

Authors such as Flecha (2008) and Flecha and Puigvert (2010) studied the prevention of gender violence from a sociological perspective, in which the elimination of violent models in force in society is encouraged, where male attraction is associated with the violence detected through ethical language and the language of desire. The premise lies in re-establishing a new masculine model where security indicates attraction (National Center for Educational

Innovation, 2015). These same authors define the term "language of desire" as the language used by young people and adolescents based on fun, passion and emotion. In contrast, the language of ethics is the language used in the family and at school, based on what is good or bad.

The model associated with attraction and violence combines relationships of the affective type with men of superiority considered sexually attractive, by using dishonest behaviors, infidelity and emotional immaturity. For Aubert, Melgar and Valls (2011, as cited in National Center for Educational Innovation, 2015), the new model encourages the establishment of a masculine behavior of equality, security and respect and is associated with passion and attraction.

In this respect, a problem based on self-esteem is reaffirmed, as there is a lack of self-knowledge and latent communication deficiencies. It is essential to practice self-acceptance, self-esteem and self-confidence, one of the challenges at the individual level in today's society, as well as to understand the concept of love with dimensions that go beyond the utopias and misconceptions that have been transmitted by the media. To understand human imperfection is to be aware of the continuous work required to live together in peace.

It is therefore important to work on the construction of a positive masculinity through critical success factors so that men stop using violence, employing factors such as sensitization, culture and education for peace, and the teaching and practice of nonviolence and the acquisition of cognitive skills for the peaceful management and transformation of their conflicts.

Women and peace

From the perspective of gender and the culture of peace, women have been situated as figures of peace due to the ancient construction of the female gender. This premise is reviewed and two proposals are presented below with the aim of improving couple and family relationships in order to favor a culture of peace.

The concept of women as peace-building agents comes from the attribution that culture has given to the female gender since ancient times, where they have been marked with the concept of

178 Culture of peace

the maternal, the ethics of care and beings-for-others with no identity for themselves other than to work, feel and think about others (Díez & Mirón, 2004). It is a connection that is naturally generated between a mother and her children, by carrying them in her womb for nine months, which thus led to the erroneous idea of females being the sex that has the total responsibility for the children.

Continuing with the theme of gender construction that has been followed for millennia, differential gender socialization distributes behaviors and roles that women and men should adopt within society. The role of women was to educate the children and take care of the home. Their behavior was not to express security nor decision-making. On the contrary, it was to be abnegated, submissive, sweet and understanding (Gallego, 2015).

The behaviors suggested by gender socialization are an example of inequality, which insists on and promotes power conflict between the couple. On the one hand, in the cognitive sphere, women are assigned the obligation to create intellectual deficiencies that do not allow them to excel in different environments, with the only one to stand out being the man; on the other hand, the behavior assigned to men is to be decisive and firm, be recognized as the head of the family—a point that was addressed earlier—to be the person in charge of making decisions, supporting the family financially and also to be obeyed (see Figure 5.4).

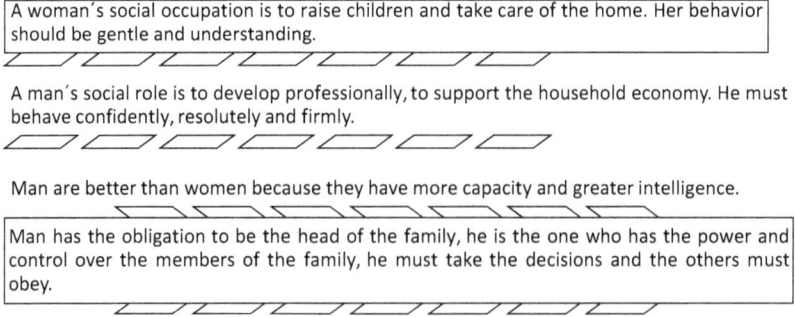

Figure 5.4 Gender-differentiated socialization.

Source: Own elaboration based on Gallego (2015).

These beliefs have become part of society in the form of a disease that has generated problems of self-esteem, which are reflected in the emotional violence that exists within marriage. It is evident that this problem has emotional roots, as both men and women are restricted from living freely, expressing themselves and developing in the way they choose, generating emotional wounds that are expressed in behaviors of frustration, dissatisfaction and anger at the way in which they have led their lives, ways that have not been decided by themselves but by following certain rules and social roles in which there was no democratic process for establishing them.

Continuing with this subject, the ideology of women as an element of passivity, related to stability, is of Greek origin. In contrast, men are dynamic, with characteristics of mobility in public action, giving rise to the freedom of men, with the consequences from men fall on women (Díez & Mirón, 2004). The same authors observe that within the family, after becoming a mother, the woman becomes a born conflict regulator, due to the practice of the ideal qualities that have been attributed to her and inherited from the female gender, such as patience, care, compassion and empathy toward the weak, all of these indispensable values and behaviors in the peaceful resolution of conflicts. Women are enriched by the natural abilities that are sometimes potentiated after becoming a mother, which are not specific to one sex or gender, since every human being has the capacity to acquire the tools of mediation, negotiation and reconciliation (see Figure 5.5).

One of the objectives of the school of thought related to alternative methods of conflict resolution is to teach society that everyone is capable of acquiring tools of dialogue in order to choose to be figures of peace, regardless of the sex in which they were born. The

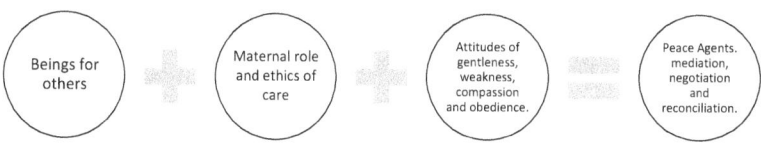

Figure 5.5 Women as agents of peace.
Source: Own elaboration based on Gallego (2015).

proposal made by authors Díez & Mirón (2004) suggests homogeneous maternal thinking for a culture of peace, which is not exclusive to women, but is also characteristic of men; therefore, they suggest the elimination of the ancestral bond that unites only the mother with the child, indicating that the work of upbringing is also the work of men, which corresponds to the idea of peace in which men and women have the same responsibility for building it.

It is often perceived that the rules of nature have provided a solution to an appropriate gender construction, an answer that has not been chosen by the majority of people. Education and responsibility within marriage and for the children is a matter of two persons; it is a responsibility for providing equal care. Another of the proposals related to the prevention of violence within the couple is to promote the acquisition of essential skills in attraction, choice and equality from childhood. These proposals are described based on Flecha, Puigvert and Redondo (2005), with a description of each of the competencies:

- Competence in attraction: this means understanding that love has a social origin, so it requires adopting an individual definition that accepts love linked with respect, union linked with passion, and rejects any person who manifests contrary behavior.
- Competence in choice: this refers to knowing how to establish affective relationships with people who provide peace, tranquility and to eliminate any connection that fosters violence, possession or domination.
- Competence in equality: this is being able to identify the social hierarchy that is in force and to establish equality through awareness, with the aim of setting up different patterns and not continuing with reproducing traditional systems of power.

These competences indicated by Flecha, Puigvert and Redondo are considered appropriate in light of the problem of inequality that has been expressed previously. A better understanding of the feeling of love is needed, which has been distorted and confused, creating emotional dependence and toxic relationships.

Another interesting perspective would be on the acquisition of emotional intelligence skills, which have their central point in the theme of high individual valuation, promoting introspection from childhood, self-observation for the recognition of natural talents that allow a person to generate a healthy, balanced and conscious self-esteem, which can result in the rejection of any violent behavior of the partner, within either marriage or society.

Toward a culture of peace in marriage

The last section of the theoretical framework aims to merge the concepts of the culture of peace and marriage by reviewing the objectives of the culture of peace, analyzing thoroughly the classifications of types of couples that exist and making proposals linked to the ethics of care and the individual components that favor the culture of peace in order to obtain an imperfect peace.

It is essential to remember that one of the aims of the culture of peace, according to Fried Schnitman (2000, as cited in Cabello, 2012), is to learn to live together. Human beings are conflictive by nature, so it is a challenge and a constant task to maintain balance and harmony within relationships, which is why values such as respect and tolerance must be drawn on, in order to live together peacefully.

Maintaining a relationship of peaceful coexistence within marriage is not a simple task; it involves not only learning components of respect and tolerance, but also of managing and controlling emotions, especially anger. Acquiring components of communication and emotional intelligence that favor a culture of peace and promote spaces of harmony within an affective relationship is one of the challenges that should be included in basic education.

According to Charny (1996, as cited in Karson 2016), six classifications of couples can be established within marriage. In order to understand the conflicts that arise within a marriage, it is essential to identify the areas where problems are generated, to implement proposals for peaceful coexistence and restore the balance; therefore, the following is a reference to the classifications of couples:

- Lovers: this refers to the area where attraction and sex predominate.
- Friends: there is solidarity, trust, listening to each other and mutual acceptance; there is no need to change each other.
- Financial partners: both manage income in a positive way, maintaining effective communication.
- Partners: two people have common interests and activities; it is not as close as a friendship, but they share pleasant moments together.
- Roommates: they have clear agreements about maintaining the home, cleaning and doing housework. There is an equal and satisfactory delegation of duties for the domestic area.
- Co-parenting: this is a positive and efficient collaboration in the upbringing of the children.

Problems arise, according to Charny, when the discomfort caused by a lack of action is not expressed clearly, directly and without aggression for one of the members of a couple, generating an imbalance and creating continuous complaints. One proposal is therefore to detect the categories of problems and keep them in compartmentalized so as not to combine conflicts.

Coexistence and conflicts are associated with emotions and feelings. Anger, fear, pain and guilt are emotions that can be triggered at any time because a person's interests are exposed; it gives rise to emotions to produce a response. In contrast, feelings provide a balance within the monitoring of the goals that you have. When the physiological alteration is high in situations where a person feels attacked, he or she immediately has the need to act and return the offense. Within affective or social relationships, when the emotional core is activated with negative feelings such as irritation or anger, the results make it difficult to solve the problem because the tendency is to act destructively as a form of protection (Acosta, 2004).

What Charny points out one of the reasons why it is mentioned that violence has a bilateral effect. When starting a cycle of verbal violence, whether either of the spouses initiates it, whether male or female, both will at some point be immersed in a violent game, where one member of the couple begins and the other follows. This is where it is suggested to use the components that favor the culture of peace, to practice assertive language, frustration tolerance and active listening as catalysts and providers of care within the marriage, favoring the culture of peace. For this type of regulation of feelings to exist, some authors indicate the way of following three paths. Taking Acosta (2004) as a reference, a description of such a proposal is made as follows:

The first step is *communication between parties and empathy*: experts point out that without productive communication and empathy, negotiation cannot take place. It requires active listening, focused attention on the problem, and an attitude of respect and trust in the other party. It is essential to work on the problem, explore what caused the disagreement and not respond with criticism or offense in order to make the objectives that generated the incompatibility more flexible, being certain that it can be overcome in a creative and participative way to the satisfaction of both parties.

The second step is the *self-regulation of anger*. Anger manifests itself when there is a perception that someone is causing a grievance or humiliation, so when the physiological mechanism is altered, there is a tendency to attack. It is therefore recommended to take a pause in order to obtain calm and tranquility. Second, it is necessary to reflect on the consequences of reacting negatively.

The third step is to analyze value conflicts, the nature of the conflict, which may be:

- Concrete: these types of conflicts are not so real; agreements can be reached quickly.
- Symbolic: these are conflicts that are usually hidden and are highly moral or sentimental. The concern is losing against the adversary and not achieving what is required.
- Transcendent: its characteristic is the incompatibility of values. Making changes or giving in is fundamental for its resolution. Conflicts of this type that have been going on for a long time, the question arises as to whether it is advisable to continue making efforts to manage the conflict.

Conflict education is indispensable if, as authors who study conflict suggest, human beings are troublesome and communicative by nature. Therefore, teaching processes should consider these two aspects together with education in values, emotional education and in the culture of peace, to develop in students socio-cognitive tools that allow them to deal positively with their conflicts and transform them through peaceful means. These teaching processes should not only be carried out by educational institutions, but should also be reinforced by social actors and other socializing institutions.

The care

Another proposal for the development of gender equality and the reduction of violence is the ethic of care, an ideology that has been developed by Spanish researchers and is described in this section, and is intended to be propagated as another constructivist alternative for peace research within marriage.

The ethic of care is a philosophy based on sharing the work of care between men and women, through the principles of justice, happiness and self-realization. To make this possible, it is necessary to reconceptualize some central aspects of social organization such as work, education and citizenship (Jiménez & Muñoz, 2012). The concept of care ethics is related to the development of the tools, values and behaviors of empathy, patience, responsibility, perseverance, commitment, listening and tenderness. These are fundamental tasks for human development, as they become the ideal way to generate satisfaction in the basic needs of affection and emotional support that all humans require (Comins, 2010). The same author points out that from the perspective of the ethics of care, conflict resolution is aimed at ensuring that neither party loses. Caring implies listening to different thoughts and being sensitive to the needs of others, in order to find satisfactory solutions for all.

The win-win outcome is a type of negotiation that is intended to be achieved not only in the ethic of care but also in the teaching of conflict resolution presented by the alternative methods school of thought. It is a new alternative to justice in which a conflict can be resolved by the parties themselves. An agreement is reached in which both parties obtain a balanced and satisfactory outcome.

Vicent Martínez (n.d., as cited in Muñoz, 2012) proposes a new communication model based on the ethics of discourse, equality and freedom in order to help people reach understanding through communication and empathy; comprehension that everyone is equal and has the same right to listen and be listened to. Vicent Martínez points out the importance of the freedom to express opinions, thoughts, feelings or emotions, emphasizing the relevance of interpretation, the responsibility of the receiver because it is the element by which it is verified that the message has been delivered and decoded correctly, so it can be addressed a type of communicative solidarity, in which its principles are sustained in the responsibility of the sender and receiver.

Expression, perception and interpretation are notable in making conflict. Establishing adequate communication favors peaceful means, while a lacking and inadequate way of communicating can provoke violent situations (Muñoz, 2012). In order to establish new relationships, authors such as Bar-Tal, Halperin and de Rivera (2007, as cited in Bar-Tal et al., 2011) indicate that in the affective domain, two related processes are required: as a first part the reduction of fear and hatred; as a second part, the need to create hope, trust and mutual acceptance.

The development of peace involves as a first step, the reformulation of objectives such as peaceful coexistence and cooperation with the old enemy, including stopping suffering, quarrels, disputes, to give the opportunity for time to give rise to tranquility. As a second step, it requires the acquisition of new skills such as negotiation, mediation, compromise, giving in and reciprocity (Jarymowics & Bar-Tal, 2006, as cited in Bar-Tal et al., 2011). These authors indicate that the peace-builder is strong, which consists of reciprocal recognition and acceptance, sharing the same interest in and commitment to developing a peaceful relationship and awareness of the other, through a positive attitude, acting as a means to develop trust. Interestingly, Jarymowics and Bar-Tal address the issue of reconciliation, an action that is unlikely to be replicated within the couple when complex events occur. It is also emphasized that these authors go back to the basic processes of assertive communication where active listening and assertive language are involved: it is the same language that has the characteristics of really expressing what one thinks in a sincere way. The ethics of care reaffirms the attention that should be given to the couple, to the treatment of daily coexistence, which requires effort every day because it is an imperfect process, which has no end.

Toward an imperfect and neutral peace in marriage

In personal, interpersonal and intrapersonal relationships, human nature is complex, conflictive and communicative, so an individual is continually in the process of learning. Within marriage, within the coexistence of two people, it cannot be different; therefore, if it could be classified into two types of peace, it would be neutral peace and imperfect peace.

Within neutral peace there are two premises on which the concept is based in order to be understood. Taking Jiménez (2014) as a reference, these premises are described as follows:

- The first is that there are no people who are neutral; therefore, there are no neutral societies, so one of the functions is to be able to neutralize people, spaces and violence in order to be at peace, since neutrality is where it resides.
- The second is that, in order to be able to neutralize conflict, for neutral peace, respect for the other is required. In this way it is possible to reduce certain types of violence.

Jiménez indicates that neutrality must be understood as a continuous search to find creative solutions to transforming conflicts, and in this way identify other options that do not provoke confrontations and generate violence. Therefore, within marriage, it is vital to carry out exercises to be able to neutralize the person, first individually, in order to find the respect that we deserve as beings. For this respect to exist, it is necessary to know and accept oneself as a whole, and for this type of process to take place, self-knowledge is indispensable. Once this process has begun, it will be easier to respect others and to use creativity to transform conflicts.

The concept of imperfect peace within gender implies detecting spaces and instances where actions can be created to generate peace, which could be a category of analysis to deal with conflicts, to facilitate people's potentialities and to build peace. Muñoz and Jiménez (2010) note that imperfect gender peace is fundamental for the devolution of power to women, who have the potential to develop conflict regulation skills. For their part, men have the task of assuming loving and caring attitudes, collaboration and the ideology of equality (Muñoz & Jiménez, 2010).

Below, taking Jiménez & Muñoz (2012) as a reference, some of the reasons why this type of peace is proposed within marriage are mentioned:

- Imperfect peace does not have an end but rather is a kind of peace that is considered and worked on daily by an actor, in some space and time. It cannot be otherwise because change is a constant, society and conflicts evolve, which is the reason for peace from the imperfect perspective.
- Imperfect peace is rooted in the complexity of the human being, starting from two approaches: the first one is that all realities have plots that are difficult to understand in their totality and, the second is that the human being has certain limitations to discern, explain or understand particular things, which is directly related to imperfection.

That is why the perspective of imperfect peace in the field of marriage does not have an end. Instead, it presents complex issues such as persuasion to the couple. Its ideology is based on work, action and continuous learning with oneself and with others to maintain balance. As described by Comins and Muñoz (2013, as cited in Coca et al., 2015), peace is something open in terms of feeling, thinking, doing and saying, which generates an imperfect vital coherence (see Figure 5.6).

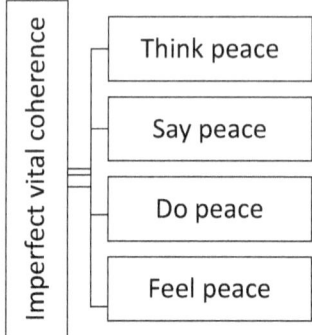

Figure 5.6 The practice of peace through imperfect coherence.
Source: Own elaboration based on Coca, García, Martín, & Ramírez (2015).

Below, taking Coca et al. (2015) as a reference, the meaning of each concept is described:

- **To think in peace**: to reason strongly, openly, to think in a way that deconstructs violence and integrates with the holistic perspective.
- **Saying peace:** to speak with authenticity, clarity, simplicity, open argumentation and affective communication between people.
- **Making peace:** to give, connect, mediate, cooperate and negotiate.
- **Feeling peace:** to feel commitment, detachment, affection, humility and care.
- **The time factor for change**: everything is gradual, and it cannot be established how long it will take; everything needs time.
- **The relevance of self-knowledge**, to generate empathy, patience, care for oneself first, and then to offer it to others.

A holistic structure of peace is presented, which is perceived as aligned with inner peace, which is within the second generation of peace. The creation of imperfect coherence points to the logic that must first exist in the individual, and then be generated and reflected in the affective relationships that develop in his or her life.

The perpetuation of the gender construction that has been maintained for generations is not perceived to have been the most favorable for a culture of peace within couple relationships. The set of behaviors that distinguish the feminine from the masculine without being questioned have generated conflicts over power and confusion that have been the ideal means to violence. In this sense, both men and women have natural characteristics and abilities, which should be used to generate balance in their union, in this case within marriage.

Nature from a sexual perspective provides men with the ability to give and women with the ability to receive, and this aspect can be applied in everyday life. The promotion of gender equity does not intend to identify men as perpetrators and women as victims, what it promotes is to give back to women their cognitive value and professional development and to men the opportunity to establish a stronger connection with their children, promoting the principles of the ethics of care, the control of words, attention in listening and calm in the face of adversity as a form of teamwork that favors the construction of peace.

Children and the new generation of peace

The importance of marriage as a cell of society is a matter that is continually highlighted throughout this book, and this is due to the social repercussions of the patterns inherited from parents to children. Imitation as a natural way of learning for children generates a critical responsibility for upbringing, a fact that parents may not consciously visualize.

The field of psychology has focused on the study of the relationship that exists between parents and children. This has been the case since World War II when research indicated the effects of the absence of parents on the mental health of children. However, it was not until the 1960s that the theory of attachment was proposed, with the work of Bowlby and Ainsworth, who explained the importance of this affective bond and considered it a fundamental need of human beings. Authors such as Álvares (2016, as cited in Bennett et al., 2021) point out that attachment is a very intense, long-lasting affective bond that emerges from the child toward the person who cares for him or her, on whom his or her safety and protection depends, and whose characteristic is that it requires physical and emotional closeness, especially in stressful situations.

The attachment theory is an example of a primordial and basic relationship in childhood. The affective bond between parents and children must be understood as an aspect of vital importance for the development of a society that intends to generate peaceful human beings who can understand conflict as natural and transform it in a positive way for learning without violence.

Among everything that has been covered in this book, the main message that we want the reader to cling to, is to understand that peace will never work in marriage if one does not continuously work on oneself. It is the process of self-knowledge that will allow the development and execution of communication skills that will provide a better understanding of oneself, a higher self-esteem and therefore a better relationship with one's partner.

Another point for reflection is the aspect of the relevance of women as the pillar of the family. Women are the only vehicle of creation, at least in a natural way, in the reproduction of the human being. For women, it is necessary to understand the importance of being well, as emotional beings, to opt for the continuous search for the teaching of well-being, for the development of skills and knowledge that allow them to find balance in all aspects of themselves, in order to be well, first, for themselves and then for their family, their children. A marriage will only be a consequence, whether positive or negative, of the state of one's physical, mental and spiritual health.

For their part, men need to work on the development of their awareness of family, on what it means to be a husband, to be a father committed to the relationship with and upbringing of children. It is therefore essential to continue promoting the type of masculinity that allows men to feel good about being fragile, sensitive, emotional and sentimental, individuals who can express themselves freely without being judged. It is through education that programs need to be implemented to free them from the ancestral burden that they are perceived to be carrying and which does not allow them to develop in a healthy way in terms of what it means to be a human being.

In conclusion, women and men are invited to initiate a process of individual healing and to be aware of the responsibility to heal as a married couple, in order to grow together, because children and the next generations will be the result of the peace that their parents achieve or fail to achieve in their relationship as a couple.

You have finished this book. Thank you.

Enjoy the experience of life in peace.

Reflection questions

1. What is peace?
2. What is a culture of peace?
3. What is the key to making peace?
4. What are the three dimensions of violence according to Johan Galtung?
5. What are positive, negative and neutral peace?
6. What are the generations of peace?
7. What is a gender perspective?
8. Describe the three types of masculinities.
9. Are women natural-born agents of peace? Justify your answer.
10. What does peace in future generations depend on?

References

Acosta Mesas, A. (2004). Regulación de conflictos y sentimientos. En B. Molina Rueda, & F. Muñoz, *Manual de Paz y Conflictos* (págs. 202–22). Granada: Universidad de Granada.

Bar-Tal, D., Rosen, Y., & Nets-Zehngut, R. (2011). Educación para la paz en las sociedades implicadas en conflictos prolongados y resistentes a su resolución: objetivos, condiciones y direcciones. En D. Páez Rovira, C. Martín Beristain, J. González-Castro, N. Basabe Barañano, & J. de Rivera, *Superando la violencia colectiva y construyendo la cultura de paz* (págs. 495–535). Madrid: Fundamentos.

Bennett Escalona, A., Hernandez Cedeño, E., & Lopez Bauta, A. (2021). Relación de apego del niño con sus padres en el primer año de vida. *Universidad de la Habana*.

Cabello Tijerina, P. (2012). *La mediación como política social aplicada al fortalecimiento de la cultura de paz en México y España*. Recuperado el 27 de abril de 2016, de DIGITUM Biblioteca Universitaria: https://digitum.um.es/xmlui/handle/10201/28093

Calderón Concha, P. (2009). *Teoría de conflictos de Johan Galtung.* Recuperado el 27 de abril de 2016, de Revista de paz y conflictos: www.ugr.es/~revpaz/tesinas/rpc_n2_2009_dea3.pdf

Centro Nacional de Innovación Educativa. (2015). *Bases de la socialización preventiva de la violencia de género.* Recuperado el 26 de abril de 2016, de Socialización preventiva de la violencia de género: https://metodologiainclusiva.files.wordpress.com/2015/11/17146.pdf

Coca Villar, C.E., García Vallinas, E., Martín Solbes, V.M., & Ramírez Hurtado, C. (2015). *Estudios en cultura de paz, conflictos, educación y derechos humanos.* Madrid: Sintesis.

Comins Mingol, I. (2010). *Coeducación en el cuidar: aportaciones para la paz.* Barcelona: Icaria.

Comins Mingol, I. (12 de febrero de 2015). *La Educación como herramienta de transformación social.* Recuperado el 9 de mayo de 2016, de YouTube: www.youtube.com/watch?v=GwZufALjLok

Díez Jorge, M. E., & Mirón Pérez, M. D. (2004). Una paz femenina. En B. Molina Rueda, & F. Muñoz, *Manual de Paz y Conflictos* (págs. 68–93). Granada: Universidad de Granada.

Díez Jorge, M. E., & Sánchez Romero, M. (2010). La construcciòn de la cultura de paz desde la perspectiva del género. En M. Alcañiz Moscardó, *Género y paz* (págs. 111–28). Barcelona: Icaria.

Flecha, A., Puigvert, L., & Redondo, G. (diciembre de 2005). *Socialización preventiva de la violencia de género.* Recuperado el 26 de abril de 2016, de Feminismos: http://rua.ua.es/dspace/bitstream/10045/3184/1/Feminismos_6_08.pdf

Flecha García, R. (26 de abril de 2016). *Nuevas masculinidades alternativas: la nueva revolución en las relaciones de género.* Conference at Universidad de Granada.

Fernández Poncela, A. M. (2010). *Mensajes didáctico-morales de la masculinidad.* Recuperado el 1 de mayo de 2017, de Masculinidades, Género y Derechos Humanos: http://200.33.14.34:1033/archivos/pdfs/Var_31.pdf

Gallego Noche, B. (2015). La Cultura de paz y la atribución de género: análisis de estructuras sociales y culturales sobre las que se mantiene la desigualdad. En C. E. Coca Villar, E. García Vallinas, V. M. Martín Solbes, & C. Ramírez Hurtado, *Estudios en cultura de paz, conflictos, educación y derechos humanos.* (págs. 27–44). Madrid: Sintesis.

García Delgadillo, J., & Mendizábal Bermúdez, G. (enero-junio de 2015). *Análisis jurídico de la paternidad con perspectiva de género: una visión desde la masculinidad.* Recuperado el 1 de mayo de 2017, de Revista latinoamericana de derecho social: www.scielo.org.mx/scielo.php?script=sci_arttext&pid=S1870-46702015000100031

Hernández Castillo, G. D. (2017). *Reconstrucción de la masculinidad.* México: Editorial Flores.

INEGI. (2014). *Estadísticas a propósito del dia de la familia mexicana.* Recuperado el 4 de noviembre de 2016, de INEGI: www.inegi.org.mx/saladeprensa/aproposito/2016/familia2016_0.pdf

Jimenez, B. F. (2014). Paz neutra: Una ilustración del concepto. *Revista de paz y conflictos,* 19–52.

Jiménez Arenas, J. M., & Muñoz, F. A. (2012). *Cultura de Paz, Conflictos, Educación y Derechos Humanos*. Granada: GEU.
Jiménez Bautista, F. (2009). *Saber pacífico: la paz neutra*. Loja, Ecuador: UTPL.
Jiménez Bautista, F. (2011). *Racionalidad pacífica. Una introducción a los estudios para la paz*. Madrid: Dykinson.
Jiménez Bautista, F. (5 de mayo de 2016). La cuarta generación de la paz. (C. S. DLa Rosa-Vazquez, Entrevistador)
Karson, M. (abril de 5 de 2016). *6 Relationships in Every Marriage*. Recuperado el 29 de abril de 2016, de Psychology Today: www.psychologytoday.com/blog/feeling-our-way/201604/6-relationships-in-every-marriage
Lado Delgado, I. (2002). La edad del matrimonio: perfectas casadas del XVIII. En P. Pérez Cantó, & M. Ortega López, *Las edades de las mujeres* (págs. 265–76). Madrid: Universidad Autónoma de Madrid.
López Martínez, M. (2004). *Enciclopedia de Paz y Conflictos*. Granada: Universidad de Granada.
Martínez Guzmán, V. (2010). Nuevas masculinidades y cultura de paz. En M. Díez Jorge, & M. Sánchez Romero, *Género y paz* (págs. 291–313). Barcelona: Icaria.
Martínez Guzmán, V., Galtung, J., Aguirre, M., Cortina, A., Skelly, J., Sanders, J., ... Fabrega Antolí, S. (1995). *Teoría de la Paz*. Valencia: Filosofía Práctica.
Martínez Hincapié, C. (2015). *De nuevo a la vida. El poder de la no violencia y las transformaciones culturales*. Bogotá: Trillas.
Ministerio de la Mujer y Desarrollo Social. (2009). *Introducción a la Cultura de Paz*. Lima, Perú: Trama.
Muñoz, F. (2012). *Comunicación y Cultura de Paz*. Granada: Editorial Universidad Granada.
Muñoz, F. A. (2004). La Paz. En B. Molina Rueda & F. A. Muñoz, *Manual de Paz y Conflictos* (págs. 25–41). Granada: Universidad de Granada.
Muñoz, F. A., & López Martínez, M. (2000). El re-conocimiento de la paz en la historia. En F. Muñoz, & M. López Martínez, *Historia de la Paz. Tiempos, espacios y actores* (págs. 15–49). Granada: Universidad de Granada.
Muñoz Muñoz, F., & Jiménez Arenas, J. (2010). Historia de una paz imperfecta de género. En M. Diez Jorge, & M. Sánchez Romero, *Género y paz* (págs. 179–218). Barcelona: Icaria .
Muñoz Muñoz, F. A., & Jiménez Arenas, J. M. (2015). Paz imperfecta y empoderamiento pacifista. En P. Cabello Tijerina, & J. Moreno Aragón, *Diversas miradas, un mismo sentir: cominicación, ciudadanía y paz como retos del siglo XXI* (págs. 49–65). Saltillo: Plaza Valdés.
Reid, A., Phillips, T., Barnes, H., Martí, F., Martínez Guzmán, V., Barnes, H., ... Zabaleta, G. (2002). *Claves para hacer las paces*. Barcelona: elkarri.
Sánchez Vázquez, L. (2010). Una Aproximación al movimiento asociativo andaluz desde la cultura de paz. En L. Sánchez Vázquez, & J. Codorníu Solé, *Movimiento Asociativo y Cultura de Paz. Una mirada desde Andalucía* (págs. 11–53). Granada: Universidad de Granada .

Index

ABCDE model 149
active listening 46, 50–1, 104, 110–14, 116, 119, 121, 123, 127, 156, 183, 186
aggressive communication 50
alternative dispute resolution (ADR) prologue 12–13
alternative solution 6, 137
anthropological models 16
assertive language 46, 50–1, 77, 93, 94, 123, 150, 156, 183, 186

baby boomer 65, 76
belief systems 61, 149, 172
Bible 7
Book of Genesis 7
brain block 55

CNDH see National Human Rights Commission (México) 63
cognitive 82, 83, 98, 121, 136, 141, 142, 144, 172, 177–89
Comins, Irene 172, 184, 187
conflicts 1, 4–6, 15–6, 22–6, 28, 32, 35, 45, 49, 54–6, 81, 87, 89, 97, 104, 111, 112, 117, 124, 155, 156, 163, 168, 172, 177, 179, 181, 184, 186, 187
conservative 15, 53, 67
construction of a culture of peace 4, 22, 54, 162
cooperation 1, 4, 10, 14, 27–30, 34, 40–4, 48, 50, 154, 160, 168, 185
Cro-Magnon man 77
culture of peace in marriage 13, 50, 181
culture of peace 4, 5, 7, 8, 13, 14, 16–18, 21–4, 27–30, 33, 44–6, 48, 50–2, 54, 55, 57, 58, 64, 67, 82, 89, 93, 110, 113, 115, 121, 127, 137, 139, 151, 154, 156, 157, 159–62, 165, 168–70, 172–5, 177, 180, 181, 183, 184, 189, 191

Dalai Lama 24
Delta 11
dialogue 1, 4, 7, 14–16, 23, 31, 32, 34, 44, 46, 48, 50–3, 57, 82, 86, 89, 90, 97, 99, 120, 124, 130, 147, 160, 162, 164, 165, 173, 179
Diaz-Guerrero's, Rogelio 58
DIF see National System for Integral Family Development 20, 21

Eirene 155
emotional intelligence (EI) 135
empathy 1, 4, 5, 7, 14, 16, 24, 44, 50, 51, 99, 110, 123, 151, 155, 161, 164, 165, 179, 183–5, 188
ENDIREH see National Survey on the Dynamics of Household Relationships
ephesians 7
equally 4, 59

fibromyalgia 60
fidelity 6
first cell 6
Freud, Sigmund 132

Galtung, Johan 5, 55, 99, 155, 163, 166
gender 154
generation 5, 6, 10, 37, 44, 65–8, 119, 122, 157–9, 163, 165–9, 188, 189
God 6
Goleman, Daniel 49, 121–3

Index   195

goodness of marriage 6
Gottman, John Mordechai 88, 89

harmful practices 42
Holmes-Rahe scale 140, 152
humanistic 1, 4
human rights 1, 4, 19, 20, 22, 23, 26, 28, 29, 31, 40, 48, 156, 160, 162, 166, 168

imperfect peace 166
INEGI *see* National Institute of Statistics and Geography
INMUJERES *see* National Institute for Women
Institute for Social Security and Services for State Workers 143
internal war 17, 24
ISSSTE *see* Institute of Social Security and Social Services for State Workers

Jiménez, Francisco 163

Levinger, George 51
lifestyles 1, 4, 39, 44, 57, 144
linguistics 78, 85, 98

Mac Gregor, Felipe 157
marriage 1, 4–10, 13, 14, 16, 19–22, 42, 45, 46, 50-2, 58–65, 68, 77, 79, 80, 84, 86, 88–91, 93, 99, 109, 110, 112, 113, 121, 131, 137, 141, 146, 151, 154, 156, 159, 169–71, 173, 179–81, 183, 184, 186, 187, 189, 190, 193
Martínez Guzmán, Vicent 185
Matrem muniens 5
meditate 17
millennial generation 67
multi-/inter-/transcultural peace 166
Muñoz, Francisco A. 163

National Human Rights Commission (México) 63
National Institute of Statistics and Geography 62, 63, 173
National Institute for Women 20
National Survey on the Dynamics of Household Relationships 63
National System for Integral Family Development 20, 21

National Institute for Clinical Excellence 120
negative peace 5, 163–5
neurolinguistic programming 98–101
neurolinguistic 98
neutral peace 163-7, 186
NICE *see* National Institute for Clinical Excellence
NLP *see* neurolinguistic programming
NOM-190 18
non violent 15M 158

Official Journal of the Federation 19, 20, 53
old psychological structure 57
Omicron 11, 12

paleonthropologists 77
pandemic 10–13, 16, 17, 35–40
paralinguistic codes 82
passive communication 50
paternal lineage 6
peaceful dialogue 7
peaceful solutions 14
peace 4, 10, 13, 18, 21, 34, 44, 45, 48, 51, 67, 89, 100, 119, 121
personal skills 7
premenstrual syndrome (PMS) 120
proxemics 126
psychological structure 57, 58, 60, 63, 64

RAE *see* Royal Spanish Academy
Redorta, Josep 141
Resolution of conflicts 23, 111, 124, 179
Rosenzweig, Saul 47
Royal Spanish Academy 132

Saint Augustine 6, 7
Saint Thomas 6
Saltillo, Coahuila 62
SARS-CoV2 10, 11, 16
SEGOB 20
Seville Manifesto 1, 4, 158
solidarity 1, 4, 14, 16, 22, 23, 27–9, 48, 50, 64, 112, 124, 154, 182, 185
Solzhenitsyn, Alexandr 51
spiritual guide 7
syntax 77

taboo 53, 58
tactesics 126
tolerance to frustration (FT) 47, 48, 130, 145, 150

UNESCO *see* United Nations Educational Scientific and Cultural Organization
United Nations Educational, Scientific and Cultural Organization 4
United Nations Organization 4
United Nations 162

violence 4, 5, 7–16, 18–21, 25, 26, 28, 30, 33, 34, 36, 40, 41, 43, 45–58, 61–4, 67, 68, 72, 75, 77, 78, 80–2, 88–91, 93, 97, 99, 101, 104, 107, 109, 117, 130–3, 136, 143, 145, 147, 152, 155–60, 162–7, 169, 174, 177, 179, 180, 182, 184, 186, 188–91, 102
virus 10, 11, 35, 37

WHO *see* World Health Organization
World Health Organization 137
Wuhan 10

XYZ 96

For Product Safety Concerns and Information please contact our EU
representative GPSR@taylorandfrancis.com
Taylor & Francis Verlag GmbH, Kaufingerstraße 24, 80331 München, Germany

www.ingramcontent.com/pod-product-compliance
Lightning Source LLC
Chambersburg PA
CBHW052021290426
44112CB00014B/2322